Once upon a time there was
COLOMBIA

Once upon a time there was
COLOMBIA

DIRECTION, DESIGN AND EDITION

Benjamín Villegas

ESSAY

William Ospina

This book has been created,
edited and published in Colombia by
VILLEGAS ASOCIADOS S. A.
Avenida 82 No. 11-50, Interior 3
Bogotá, D. C., Colombia
Telephone 571.616.1788, Fax 571.616.0020
E-mail: informacion@VillegasEditores.com

© VILLEGAS EDITORES S. A. 2005

Art Department
ANDREA VÉLEZ / DAVID RENDÓN

Editorial Coordination
JUAN DAVID GIRALDO

Proofreader
STELLA FEFERBAUM

English translation
JIMMY WEISKOPF

The editor expresses his special thanks to
BANCO UNION COLOMBIANO
for the institutional sponsorship
of the present edition of this book.

All rights reserved.
No part of this book may be reproduced,
stored in a retrieval system or transmited,
in any form or by any means, electronic,
mechanical, photocopying, recording or otherwise,
without the prior permission of Villegas Editores.

First edition, October 2005

ISBN 958-8156-64-5

Pages 2-3: Mist forest, Sierra Nevada de Santa Marta.
Pages 4-5: Coral forest, Island of Providencia.
Pages 6-7: Desert of La Guajira.
Pages 8-9: Tarapaja lake, Amazon River.
Page 10: Guaitarilla, Nariño.
Pages 12-13: Canyon of the Magdalena River, Huila.
Page 15: Anthropozoomorphic mask
Tumaco Inguapi culture, 400 B.C. – 100 B.C.
29.9 x 21.6 cm. Gold Museum,
Banco de la República, Bogotá.
Pages 16-17: Tota lake, Boyacá.
Page 18: Antioquia.
Pages 20-21: Island of San Andrés.
Front cover: Cumbal, Nariño.
Back cover: Taganga, Madgalena.

VillegasEditores.com

CONTENTS

ONCE UPON A TIME THERE WAS COLOMBIA   23

THE REALM OF DIVERSITY   27

IN THE REGION OF EXCESS   43

THE INVISIBLE PAST   75

THE LESSONS LEFT BY POETRY   99

A COUNTRY OF CONTRASTS   115

A JOURNEY THROUGH COLOMBIA   137

COLOMBIA   161

CITIES AND REGIONS   185

INHABITING THE LANGUAGE   211

IN SEARCH OF COLOMBIA   245

A CENTURY'S UPHEAVALS   273

ONCE UPON A TIME THERE WAS COLOMBIA

As is the case with most of our books, the subject of this one is, once more, Colombia – the irreplaceable and permanent focus of our feelings and concerns – seen, this time, through William Ospina's profound reflections on the country's past, present and future.

The origin of this work goes back to a newspaper column the author wrote years ago, where he confessed that one of his secret dreams was to write a book about Colombia in which words and pictures would complement each other to merge into the vision of the country guarded in his mind. Although we had not yet met, his ambition coincided with an idea for a book that I had been thinking about for some time and I immediately felt in harmony with him.

So, taking the initiative, I sought him out and we got together. After an enthusiastic exchange of ideas, we agreed that he would take charge of the text for the project we had in mind and I would work on the illustrations and the design. From the very beginning I was sure that William Ospina – without doubt one of the most lucid and best-known writers and thinkers of the younger Colombian generation – would be the ideal companion on this adventure. His analysis of Colombia's future possibilities largely coincided with my own and his opinions about how our country might be able to reconcile itself with its defects and fully exploit its many advantages were convincing to me.

Although our respective commitments forced us to postpone the project, year after year, it continued to fascinate us and we never thought of abandoning it. Two years ago we got down to work: the texts began to emerge and the design to take shape. At the beginning of this year the book we had dreamt of for so long finally came together.

Regardless of where you dip into it, this book relates the history of the country in terms that go far beyond the traditional description of important events and leading figures. Ospina presents an integral vision of Colombia in which every facet is linked to the whole. Starting from the country's ancient indigenous past and rural roots, it advances towards the present reality of a largely urban and mestizo country, covering every relevant feature, from landscape and art to anthropology and history.

It is a work that offers a penetrating look at the very foundations of Colombia's idiosyncrasies and the purest expressions of its personality.

Opposite: Los Estoraques Park. Norte de Santander.

Pages 24-25: Sandoná, Nariño.

BENJAMÍN VILLEGAS

THE REALM OF DIVERSITY

In his poem *Morada al sur* (Abode in the south), Aurelio Arturo wrote that Colombia is the country where green is of all colors. Eager to refine the hues of perception in order to describe the appearance of his native valley in the south, where the fields of the smallholdings each display a different green, the poet was also suggesting the key to the fate of one of the world's most diverse countries.

What we now call Colombia (because there were other Colombias in the past and there will probably be others, different to it, in the future) is a challenge for those who think that a nation is defined by its oneness. This challenge is shared by all of America, but Mexico has a millennial indigenous profile, Argentina an astonished European profile and the Caribbean and Brazil an African profile: the smiling countenance of a mulatto race. Most of these countries essentially know who they are, know to what tradition they belong: by contrast, in recent times the fate of Colombia has been to secretly envy those which have a clear awareness of their origins and to that extent a clear idea of their destiny.

For this reason it is not strange that nowadays, at the beginning of the 21st century, the country struggles in a desperate search for its future face and that in a world that has achieved considerable progress in so many different fields, Colombia seems to have paused at the threshold of the barbarian cosmogonies, fascinated by but incapable of understanding itself, entangled in a curious fight of all against all, which, being so destructive on the battlefield, embraces many other fields as well and also manifests itself in a taut deployment of creative forces and an excessive competition among all of its components.

We could say, at least metaphorically, that in Colombia the human aspect too is of all colors and no element seems willing to subordinate itself to the others. This was already evident in the course of its history and it cannot help being significant that Colombia has been the one country in Mestizo America that has not enthusiastically marched behind dictators.

It had dictators for short periods, but every hint of dictatorship was repelled by the energetic reaction of some sector of its society, and one of the most dramatic moments of our history was precisely what is known as the abominable night of September, when, daggers in hand, some of the men who most admired him entered the house of the Liberator, Simón Bolívar, who intended to assume dictatorial powers in order to deal with the political unrest of that time. The plot failed because, with the help

Opposite:
Anthropomorphic and zoomorphic pictographs.
Tomachipán, Guainía.

Any approach to the country is an approach to a region of the world where diversity is the law in all fields of reality: it is to see a historical process where by chance – if we do not believe in the inevitable dictates of destiny – the most diverse elements converged to produce the most unpredictable results.

28   Los Katios National Natural Park. Chocó.

Opposite: Pan de Azúcar snow-covered mountain, Sierra Nevada del Cocuy. Boyacá.

If something characterizes nature here, it is its unruliness and exuberance. And if something forces us to adopt a respectful attitude to it, it is this double condition of generosity and menace.

of his mistress Manuela Sáenz, Bolívar managed to jump out of a window and find refuge in the nearby shadows of the San Francisco River, the place where we find the avenida Jiménez de Quesada today.

Almost all of the conspirators lost their lives, some in front of a firing squad and others because of their own sense of guilt, but the event made evident an attitude that would repeat itself many times in the future.

We might even point out that this attitude did not arrive with the Independence. In the times of the Conquest, the young, brave and cruel Pedro de Ursúa, trying to prove his worth to his uncle, governor Miguel Díaz de Armendáriz, with the aim of gaining permission to go in search of the fabulous treasure of the Muisca indigenous chief Tisquesusa, waged four fierce wars: one in the south against the Panches, in the blue-mountain country of Neiva; another against the Muzos, in the country of emeralds; another in the northeast against the Chitareros, behind the arid canyons of the Chicamocha river, and the last in the north against the Taironas, in the mountain range of stone-built cities and snow-covered peaks that rises alongside the Caribbean sea. And in all of them he displayed an unusual bravery and the fierceness of a tiger.

But when he returned to Santafé de Bogotá to claim his reward, he discovered that his uncle, the governor, had been removed from office and that an order for his arrest had been issued, because of his cruelty to the Indians. Ursúa, who had shortly before been the most powerful man in the Kingdom of Nueva Granada (the colonial name for Colombia), fled towards the north like an outlaw, along a river full of caimans, the Magdalena (or río grande de la Magdalena, as it was known), set sail for Panama, where he waged a cruel war against the *cimarrones* (runaway slaves) and from there traveled to Peru, where he set out on the desperate attempt to conquer the jungle of the Amazon, only to die, almost at once, at the hands of Lope de Aguirre.

Some echo of these ancient wars survives in the current conflicts of Colombia but they do not prove to us that the country's destiny is necessarily one of violence, only that our ills are ancient ones. One of them is the debility that allows each of the country's riches to provoke a war, because of the difficulty of uniting its society to protect and share those riches, and the tendency to regard large sectors of the population as a nuisance that stands in the way of the intentions of a few powerful men.

The peoples who lived around Ancient Greece used to say that every Greek was a tyrant. Perhaps this lack of a collective vocation for tyranny in Colombia reveals, instead, that every individual here has such a liking for tyranny that he is unwilling to subject himself to anyone else's tyranny. In Greece it led to the invention of democracy, since a suitable regime for a country in which everyone wants to be king is the rule of all, that is, giving each citizen his portion of power. But this consensus nevertheless requires that beyond all rivalries there should exist a common identity and it is difficult to get all Colombians to identify themselves with a single personality, truth or aesthetics. So far Colombia has never achieved a scheme of majorities and

Opposite: The Colón and Bolívar peaks, Sierra Nevada de Santa Marta, Magdalena.

Pages 32-33: The shore of the Caribbean, La Guajira peninsula.

Today, at the beginning of the 21st century, Colombia is one of the most ungovernable countries in the world and this seems strange in an age when the power of the communications media, corporations and states already appears to be limitless and is triumphing in so many places over the docility of the masses.

its revolts often inclined more to crime than politics, because the private always won out over the collective.

A Colombian wit used to say that in Colombia the revolutionary crowds always set out for the Presidential Palace, but wind up, a few hours later, looting the stores where they sell hams. Some ancient and persistent factor has prevented the triumph of political schemes with broad perspectives, and an extreme fragmentation meant that the country was always governed by partisan interests, by the designs of the most powerful and influential sectors.

In the middle of the 20th century, the political leader Jorge Eliécer Gaitán electrified crowds with his populist political program, which was expressed through impassioned speeches full of republican ideals and quotes from the Latin classics, and the country seemed ready to incorporate its ignored masses into the national legend, but Gaitán, as a lawyer, believed in the rule of law and refused to seize power by undemocratic means, and it wasn't long before a tyrannical bullet cut him down, producing the greatest frustration of hopes in the republican history of Colombia.

In the face of any statement, any truth, any prestigious name, there will always be a Colombian who vehemently denies, refutes or opposes it. This may be regarded as something hatefully negative by the enthusiasts of authority, by those who think that society is not viable if it is not founded on force; but today we can see it as a challenge for the imagination as it searches for the type of democracy in which being a citizen does not mean being an eternal subordinate, that harmless personage out of Kafka who humbly suffers the arbitrariness of the State, the petty tyranny of officials, the extravagant manipulations of the powers that be.

As we know, every problem is an opportunity. This rebellious character of Colombians, doubtless shared by many persons in the world today, may perhaps symbolize the hope that we will see a resistance to the great evils that are advancing over the planet today: the manipulation of consciences, the invasion of privacy, the gradual interference of the power structure in the internal affairs of individuals – an accusation that was formerly only leveled against certain totalitarian regimes but which is the main temptation of politics and the market today. For the moment, it is a problem for the country and if something has kept Colombian politicians awake at night in recent times it is what an awkward neologism calls governability.

Today, at the beginning of the 21st century, Colombia is one of the most ungovernable countries in the world and this seems strange in an age when the power of the communications media, corporations and states already appears to be limitless and is triumphing in so many places over the docility of the masses.

The prosperity of the United States is based on a dynamics of work and consumption, which, thanks to the communication media, does not seem to brook any opposition. The subordination to tradition and the State of the Germans or the Japanese makes those countries world powers and is responsible for their vigorous economies and

In the middle of the 20th century, the political leader Jorge Eliécer Gaitán electrified crowds with his populist political program, which was expressed through impassioned speeches full of republican ideals and quotes from the Latin classics, and the country seemed ready to incorporate its ignored masses into the national legend, but Gaitán, as a lawyer, believed in the rule of law and refused to seize power by undemocratic means, and it wasn't long before a tyrannical bullet cut him down, producing the greatest frustration of hopes in the republican history of Colombia.

Opposite: Plaza de Bolívar, Bogotá, ca. 1940.

Pages 36-37: Grove of *guadua* bamboo. Chinchiná, Caldas.

powerful armies, but it was also responsible for the horrors of Fascism and clips the wings of any truly dissident adventure by the individual.

The ritual suicide of Mishima and the madness of Hölderlin may perhaps be symbols of the limits placed on individual expression in such homogeneous cultures, but if one thing stands out in Colombia it is the individual, to the extent that being individual becomes a temptation, and it remains to be seen whether those who kill themselves or go mad here do so, not because of excessive limits on their thought but the absence of them, because of that eagerness for the absolute that may be seen in a poem that is very characteristic of the way that Colombians are, that poem by Porfirio Barba Jacob entitled:

Arrogance (*Soberbia*)

I asked him for a sublime song that would sweeten
my coarse, monotonous and harsh life,
he gave me a lark of bewitching rhyme,
I wanted a thousand.

I asked him for an example of sure rhythm
with which I might govern my zeal,
he gave me a little stream, nocturnal murmuring,
I wanted a sea.

I asked him for a bonfire of never extinguished heat
so that it would lend warmth to my dreams,
he gave me a firefly that faintly glows,
I wanted a sun.

How vain life is, how useless my urge,
and the Edenic verdure and the blue April.
Oh squalid guide on the nocturnal journey,
I want to die!

How has Colombia come to form this human type that is so diverse, so rebellious, so irreducible, in which the virtues and defects of the modern idea of individualism stand out so sharply? Any approach to the country is an approach to a region of the world where diversity is the law in all fields of reality: it is to see a historical process where by chance – if we do not believe in the inevitable dictates of destiny – the most diverse elements converged to produce the most unpredictable results.

Human types: 39
Cali, Valle del Cauca;
Bolívar, Antioquia;
Island of Providencia;
Bogotá.

Pages 40-41: Open-air drying of beans, Quindío.

We could say, at least metaphorically, that in Colombia the human aspect too is of all colors and no element seems willing to subordinate itself to the others. This was already evident in the course of its history and it cannot help being significant that Colombia has been the one country in Mestizo America that has not enthusiastically marched behind dictators.

IN THE REGION OF EXCESS

Every privilege entails challenge and danger at the same time and Colombia is a spectacularly privileged country. You have only to travel round any region to feel the splendor of nature in Colombia: its dense, bio-diverse jungles in the south and west, the sea of trees in the Amazon, the rain forests of the Pacific; the mist forests in the three cordilleras into which the Andes divide before pooling into the prairies of the Caribbean; the fertile valleys of the rivers Cauca and Magdalena, which stretch out from the Colombian Massif until they merge into the Mompox Depression; the vast fluvial prairies of the Orinoco; and those treasures of biodiversity which are the Serranía de la Macarena, the Sierra Nevada del Cocuy and the Sierra Nevada de Santa Marta.

In the jungles the close-packed trees do not let in the light of day; in the mountains the mist produces, in broad daylight, that disturbing phenomenon, the white-out, places where everything is invisible; in the hot climates the fierce rainstorms blot out the world. This oppressive dynamic of a nature which is too active, too vigorous, which is insolently fecund, was a hellish experience for the Spanish conquistadors when they penetrated the wilds of the equinoctial regions in the ingenuous belief that America would be the same as the gentle lands of Europe.

Everything was similar but nothing was the same. The Andes were not the Alps, Antioquia was not Asturias, the Caribbean was not the Mediterranean, the Amazon jungle was not the Black Forest, the boa constrictors were not the restrained serpents they knew. Here nature was the queen and its fruitfulness also partook of what the poet Álvaro Mutis has called the elements of disaster. If something characterizes nature here, it is its unruliness and exuberance. And if something forces us to adopt a respectful attitude to it, it is this double condition of generosity and menace.

A French travel agency brochure once described the country to tourists in the following terms: "if you want to know the Caribbean, travel to Cuba or the Dominican Republic; if you prefer the Pacific, go to Chile; if you are interested in the cordillera of the Andes, get to know Ecuador; if you wish to experience the Amazon jungle, go to Brazil; if you want to know about the pre-Colombian cultures, think about Mexico or Peru; but if you want to see all these things together, go to Colombia". Thus, a new proof of complexity is added to the former ones – the certainty that Colombia is a kind of synthesis of Latin America, a mosaic of the attractions and also of the problems of the continent.

Rocks of Suesca. Cundinamarca.

We are in the region of excess and this is equally evident in its abundance and its fragility. In Colombia a few days of dry weather produce water shortages and electricity cuts, while a few days of rain lead rivers to burst their banks, raze the settlements on their banks and hurl avalanches of mud onto the highways. There are few regions of the world where you need such a knowledge of the world, such a spirit of precaution, so many scruples about your relationship to nature…

44   Above: Chadó, Chocó.

Below: Güicán, Boyacá.

Opposite, above: Los Patos lake. La Guajira.

Opposite, below: Cristales stream. La Macarena, Meta.

Here the conquest of America was never-ending, because it was not only a matter of different villages and groups and geographical regions, but also different cultures, mythologies and divinities, many of which put up an unyielding resistance to the Spanish invaders.

Any part of the territory of what is today Colombia is subject to the gravitational pull of four powerful planetary forces. These influences may not be perceptible at once, because the size of the country means that the great forces which rule it are hidden from our eyes. But you only have to study Colombian nature to discover a wealth, a diversity and an abundance that would be difficult to match. Colombia is a country in which 45,000 species of plants grow. It has the greatest variety of birds in the world (1753 species), the greatest variety of amphibians (583 species), the fourth-highest variety of reptiles (475 species) and the sixth-highest variety of mammals (453 species).

Undoubtedly, it is the fact that the country receives the direct influence of the Atlantic Ocean, Pacific Ocean, the subterranean forces of the "Pacific Ring of Fire" and the Amazon jungle which produces these extremes of vitality.

We are in the region of excess and this is equally evident in its abundance and its fragility. In Colombia a few days of dry weather produce water shortages and electricity cuts, while a few days of rain lead rivers to burst their banks, raze the settlements on their banks and hurl avalanches of mud onto the highways. There are few regions of the world where you need such a knowledge of the world, such a spirit of precaution, so many scruples about your relationship to nature, and it is here where a history made of wars broke the links with the immeasurable ancestral wisdom of the indigenous people and has not known how to recover that wisdom nor replace it with a new knowledge.

We may be certain that the indigenous peoples, who had inhabited this territory for a long time, always employed the wisdom and prudence which this land required – a wisdom that was the fruit of observation and experience, elaborated in complex myths and meaningful legends and efficiently transmitted from one generation to the next. It is admirable to see today, following the patient studies of anthropologists and archaeologists, the relics of the system of canals that the Zenués developed in order to cultivate the land in their region of swamps, a subtle framework of irrigation canals that allowed them to exploit the natural irrigation of the soils and obtain agricultural benefits by minimizing the risk of floods.

Equally noteworthy was the system of land distribution employed by the Pacces in the region of the Cauca Valley, where each farming unit had access to plots in the prairie, the foothills and the cordillera, so that farming became a dialogue with the geographical complexity of that region. It is astonishing to see the system of symbolic exchanges with nature that governs the world of the U'wa of the sierra del Cocuy, a ritual order that always ensured peace with their neighbors and a sense of reverence for the earth and its material goods. It is painful to imagine how painful the conflict between the Spanish idea of nature and that of the indigenous peoples must have been at the time of the Conquest.

In a land as varied as Colombia the kind of social order reached by the native peoples seems to have always depended on topography and nature. The idea that only the

Boy of the Ingano indigenous group. Putumayo.

We may be certain that the indigenous peoples, who had inhabited this territory for a long time, always employed the wisdom and prudence which this land required – a wisdom that was the fruit of observation and experience, elaborated in complex myths and meaningful legends and efficiently transmitted from one generation to the next.

Opposite: *Chinche* bugs.

Above, left: Cicada.

Above, right: Spider.

Below, left: *Chinche* bug.

Below, right: Satyrid butterfly.

… you only have to study Colombian nature to discover a wealth, a diversity and an abundance that would be difficult to match.

50

Above, left:
Passion-flower.

Above, right:
Anthurium.

Below, left: Ginger.

Below, right:
Yellow *camarón*.

Opposite: Orchid.

Colombia is a country in which 45,000 species of plants grow.

Colombia has the greatest variety of birds in the world: 1753 species.

Above, left: Spectacled bear. Quindío.

Above, right: *Tigrillo* (South American ocelot). Amazon.

Below, left: Howler monkey. Amazon.

Below, right: Iguana. Chocó.

Opposite: Frog. Chocó.

Colombia has world´s greatest variety of amphibians (583 species), the fourth-highest variety of reptiles (475 species) and the sixth-highest variety of mammals (453 species).

Muisca nation reached a certain degree of order and higher political structure is a myth. When we look at the excellence of the ceramics of many indigenous nations and the refinement of the gold-work of the Quimbayas and Calimas, the Taironas, Zenúes and Malaganas, we have no right to assume that theirs was a barbaric world. What the Muiscas did accomplish was the conquest of some of the neighboring groups and the settlement of a land that was particularly auspicious and fertile. They thus established the third largest indigenous kingdom still in force in America at the time the Europeans arrived, whose setting was the vast savannah that is now shared by the Colombian departments of Cundinamarca and Boyacá.

During the Conquest, this realm – which never came to have the monumental architecture, expansive force or pyramidal structure of the strongest American empires, the Aztec and the Inca, nor the highly-developed astronomical science, urban planning or historical records of the refined Mayas of Central America – suffered the disappearance of notable monuments, like the temple of the sun in Sugamuxi, built with precious woods, which, according to legend, burnt for months.

The Muiscas depended on their wealth of gold, their salt mines, textiles, dense fields of maize and abundant water sources, and, like other of the country's indigenous groups, perfected a refined gold-work that turned gold into an instrument for interpreting the world: an adornment, memory and sacred language. To understand Colombia it is important to know that it was never a centralized empire like Mexico or Peru, but a collection of more than 120 different indigenous nations, with their respective languages, customs and mythologies, scattered throughout a territory of astonishing variety. The rainforest country of the Cuna and Emberá of the Chocó is very different from the country of misty mountains and peaceful villages of the Kogis and Ika of the Sierra Nevada de Santa Marta.

The jungle country of the Desana of the Vaupés is different from the open prairie country of the Sikwani of the Vichada; the country of hillsides and rivers of the U'wa of the Cocuy is different from the desert plains country of the Wayuu of the Guajira; the forest country of the Kamsá and Ingas of the Putumayo is different from the country of the cold mountain flanks of the Guambianos of Cauca, and here we only mention some of the nearly ninety surviving indigenous nations of the country, many of which are struggling to find strength in their traditions and save their languages, although it is doubtful that they will be able to achieve a demographic recuperation.

But the scenarios of the vanished cultures were also very different: the country of the *ceiba* and *hobo* trees of the Zenúes, who sowed tombs full of gold in the region of what is today the departments of Bolívar and Córdoba; or the home of the Quimbaya, the department of el Quindío in the Central Cordillera, the region of the golden warriors' helmets, a world of immense *guadua* bamboo groves and of wax palms that stand upright on the summits; or the country of the Tairona, who built cities of stone on the heights of the sierra; or the Pacific littoral of the Tumaco, who in their pottery

Opposite: Molas, fabrics with patchwork design of the Cuna indigenous group.

Pages 58-59: Man of the Arhuaco indigenous group. Sierra Nevada de Santa Marta, Magdalena.

To understand Colombia it is important to know that it was never a centralized empire like Mexico or Peru, but a collection of more than 120 different indigenous nations, with their respective languages, customs and mythologies, scattered throughout a territory of astonishing variety.

Above, left: Wayuu indigenous woman.

Above, right: Emberá indigenous woman.

Below, left: Cuna indigenous woman.

Below, right: Guambiana indigenous woman.

It was also this abundance of independent nations that made the conquest of Colombian territory longer and more arduous than that of other regions. The centralized indigenous empires yielded to the first advance of the conquistadors, but here, where there was a different group every few leagues, seizing one village never meant achieving power over the next one.

Pre-Columbian stone terraces, Sierra Nevada de Santa Marta, Magdalena.

left us representations, not only of their facial features but a great many aspects of their daily life, done with an exquisite realism and so finely drawn that some scholars have compared it to Mayan art.

The origin of all those peoples is lost in the mists of time and their diversity, which is seen in their physiognomy and racial typology, poses many problems for those who theorize about how the continent was settled, but of course it is not merely a question of an anthropological perspective, because that considerable diversity of indigenous typologies is a fundamental ingredient in the diversity of faces that we see today on the streets of our cities. Recent studies show that even the region of Antioquia, traditionally considered to be the whitest and most Spanish of the country, has a strong component of the Emberá indigenous type, which has shaped its singular physiognomy, human style and, if you like, a kind of beauty which it would be impossible to find in Europe.

It was also this abundance of independent nations that made the conquest of Colombian territory longer and more arduous than that of other regions. The centralized indigenous empires yielded to the first advance of the conquistadors, but here, where there was a different group every few leagues, seizing one village never meant achieving power over the next one. When you follow the chronicles of the different invasions of indigenous lands you encounter a number of desperate and nearly endless campaigns: the advance of Balboa through the Darién, of Bastidas along the Caribbean seaboard, of Pedro de Heredia in the Sinú, of Lebrón along the Magdalena, of Jorge Robledo through Antioquia, of Jiménez de Quesada to the savanna of Bogotá, of Federman's Germans along the eastern cordillera; of Belalcázar, who reached Popayán and Cali from the south; of Pérez de Quesada in the region of Neiva.

Here the conquest of America was never-ending, because it was not only a matter of different villages and groups and geographical regions, but also different cultures, mythologies and divinities, many of which put up an unyielding resistance to the Spanish invaders.

There were many mass suicides by indigenous communities which were unwilling to endure the destruction of their cultures and the triumph of the invaders. When we go on a Sunday outing on the savanna of Bogotá, we can still see, heading towards Sutatauza, the rocky cliffs from which a legion of Indians who refused to accept the Spanish yoke threw themselves. The custom even persists today, as in the case of the U'wa indigenous people of el Cocuy, who have threatened to undertake a mass suicide to defend their way of life from a multinational oil company which wants to drill oil on the outskirts of their reserve, a natural resource which they believe is "the earth's blood".

In Colombia there is perhaps no community which has such a sacramental view of nature as the U'wa, which more organically depends on it, and there is no doubt that they are willing to die if something which they consider to be essential to life were to

Opposite: Floating markets.
Güapi, Cauca.

Pages 64-65: Gold Museum, Bogotá.

In a land as varied as Colombia the kind of social order reached by the native peoples seems to have always depended on topography and nature.

Above, left:
Tuta, Boyacá.

Above, right:
Ráquira, Boyacá.

Below, left:
Island of San Andrés.

Below, right: La
Pedrera, Caquetá.

… The origin of all those peoples is lost in the mists of time and their diversity, which is seen in their physiognomy and racial typology, poses many problems for those who theorize about how the continent was settled, but of course it is not merely a question of an anthropological perspective, because that considerable diversity of indigenous typologies is a fundamental ingredient in the diversity of faces that we see today on the streets of our cities.

be violated. Some ancient Indian peoples, like the one known as the Panches, fought to the death; others organized periodical rebellions; and many others which had to submit to Spanish domination, at least formally, conserved a redoubt of bitter skepticism, and never interiorized the mental order that subdued them.

In Colombia you often hear talk of "malicia indígena" (indigenous maliciousness). It refers to a certain intuitive cunning that enables mestizo Colombians like ourselves to successfully get out of jams or evade responsibilities. It also signifies a knack for pretending to be pleased that helps a person to deceive others about his true intentions. In some of his novels Faulkner showed how the Blacks who were freed from slavery loved to lie and took pleasure in believing their own lies: perhaps it was a way of granting language the status of a magic substitute for an inaccessible reality, of surpassing the limitations of the real by turning words into an accomplished fact. Our indigenous maliciousness is different and, I would say, less innocent: at times it is a form of rancor, disguised as acquiescence, that lays the victim open to the killer punch. It might seem irrelevant, but it isn't when it forms a more or less generalized practice and it could be said that our well-known distrust of the law is one of the ways that a traditionally rebellious society seeks vengeance for ancestral disgraces.

When everyone swears that he respects the law but takes advantage of the slightest blink of the authorities or witnesses to break or evade it, there is something more than a legal problem at stake. And I am not speaking of the present-day indigenous communities (who are governed by and respect ancestral codes of law) but of the rest of the population, mestizos by culture or by blood. People distrust the law all over the world, but in many modern democracies this may be checked by a real effort, on the part of States, to make the letter of law coincide with its reality. Unfortunately, our culture – founded, at the outset, on so many arbitrary measures, so many acts of violence that were quickly given a divine sanction by the Church and the discourse of politicians, and full of such a profound mistrust of the validity of a legal system that was almost always shameful in early times – did not make a sufficient effort to modify the discriminatory nature of its laws and allowed a deep-rooted skepticism that is one of the central marks of our national identity to come into being.

Colombia has experienced, for a long time, the contrast between the solemn formality of the law and its weak echo in the conscience of its citizens. The critics of our juridical system are puzzled by the fact that a society which is so inclined to break the law is at the same time so concerned with legal norms, and that everything in it has to be specified by legal codes. But the more the law is broken, the more meticulous become the norms, in a desperate effort to persuade the citizen to comply with them, without realizing that the two things are complementary. Societies which are rooted in a long tradition, have kept their customs alive and respect social rituals never need to have such detailed laws, for the simple reason that custom is the law. There are countries which do not even have a written constitution and this shows the important role

Above, left: Seated figure; negative painting. Classical Quimbaya.

Above, right: Incised design. Recent Quimbaya.

Below, left: Anthropomorphic vessel; polychrome negative painting. Classical Quimbaya.

Below, right: Seated female anthropomorphic figure; polychrome negative painting. Classical Quimbaya.

Opposite: Burial mounds.
San Agustín, Huila.

Below: Tatuyo indigenous men. Piraparaná, Vaupés.

Opposite: Indigenous group wearing ceremonial attire. San Martín, Amazon.

Pages 72-73: Hypogeums, Tierradentro, Cauca.

played in them by tradition and the clear way in which the relation among individuals is governed by deeply-rooted customs.

In *One hundred years of solitude*, Gabriel García Márquez speaks of a curious epidemic of sleeplessness which causes human beings to forget everything. Its impact on awareness is so strong that people gradually forget the names and functions of things and wind up filling their lives with signs to remind them of even the most elementary facts. "The sign that hung from the neck of the cow was a perfect example of the way in which the inhabitants of Macondo were resolved to fight against forgetfulness: This is the cow, you have to milk it every morning so that it gives milk and you have to boil the milk when you put it into your coffee and make a milky coffee". If a human community has to write down all of its acts, this can only mean that it lives in an improvised mental order. Thus, the region of excess tends to be the region of the pure present, where the atemporal nature of things is more evident than human achievements, experiences and memories. The indigenous peoples, whose living universe is nature, conserve their memory in their myths. The mestizo peoples, now inscribed in history, can only renounce historical memory at the cost of living in the world in a makeshift way. From the moment that "history" irrupted into our land, our riches became a source of violence: like a character in García Márquez, we Colombians wound up dying of poverty in paradise.

The rainforest country of the Cuna and Emberá of Chocó is very different from the country of misty mountains and peaceful villages of the Kogis and Ika of Sierra Nevada de Santa Marta. The jungle country of the Desana of Vaupés is different from the open prairie country of the Sikwani of the Vichada; the country of hillsides and rivers of the U'wa of Cocuy is different from the desert country of the Wayuu of Guajira; the forest country of the Kamsá and Ingas of Putumayo is different from the cold mountain flanks of the Guambianos of Cauca, to mention only some of the nearly ninety surviving indigenous nations of the country, many of which are struggling to find strength in their traditions and save their languages, although it is doubtful that they will be able to achieve a demographic recuperation.

THE INVISIBLE PAST

From the beginning there was always some powerful thing in Colombia that encouraged forgetfulness. And it became nearly a tradition that the past would ceaselessly reemerge like an incredible surprise; everything has to be discovered all over again, as though it had never been seen before. Completely unknown ancient cultures suddenly appear, like that of Malagana on the plains of Palmira, where, in the 1990's, Colombians were dazzled by the exquisite gold-work found in their burial sites, quite different to the traditional one of other native peoples.

Or living tribes suddenly spring up in the darkness of the jungle, like the surprising Nukak Makú of the Amazon, the last surviving nomadic group of the planet's jungles, who have enabled us to see how the communities of the remote past lived and discover the wisdom of their relationship with the earth, their skill at fabricating improvised shelters, utensils and ornaments, and their harmonious family and tribal life. The discovery of the indigenous universe that existed here always took longer in Colombia than in many other parts of the continent: in fact it only took place in the past half century, which proves that, as the Colombian historian Germán Arciniegas believed, the colonial and republican culture made no effort to discover the American world but, rather, to conceal it until it became nearly imperceptible.

In the countries where it was not so easy to deny, this past persisted and came to be an important element in the construction of their republics. No one is able to erase the pyramids of the Sun and the Moon on the plains of Teotihuacán, with their polychrome bases of great ritual serpents and the fierce jaguars of their temples. No one would be able to deny the existence of the indigenous masses of Mexico and Bolivia, of the jungles of Central America and the mountains of the Incas. But when many of the great creations of such cultures are invisible, when they are only to be found in their myths, unwritten languages and customs, it is easier to erase their complexity out of contempt or oversight.

One of the hidden features of *mestizaje* (the mixing of races), when it is not the fruit of love but of violence, is the silence imposed on one of the sources of blood. Every racial mixture engendered by love has a seed of freedom and its result is joy. This fact allows us to understand the warm sensuality, happy vitality and frankness of the mulatto races of the Caribbean. But what is born of contempt sows shame about one's body, a resentment and devaluation of oneself. The little treasures of love are the seed for the solidarities of the future. As Emily Dickinson so beautifully wrote:

Opposite: Leopoldo Richter. *Watercolor* (detail), 1950. 28 x 24 cm.

Pages 76-77: Enrique Grau. *Witches' Sabbath in Cartagena* (detail), 1982. 191 x 664 cm. Cartagena Convention Center. Cartagena, Bolívar.

The discovery of the indigenous universe that existed here always took longer in Colombia than in many other parts of the continent: in fact it only took place in the past half century, which proves that, as the Colombian historian Germán Arciniegas believed, the colonial and republican culture made no effort to discover the American world but, rather, to conceal it until it became nearly imperceptible.

> By Chivalries as tiny,
> A Blossom, or a Book,
> The seeds of smiles are planted –
> Which blossom in the dark.

Opposite: Hacienda La Sierra (El Paraíso). Valle del Cauca.

Pages 80-81: Indigenous village of Nabusimake. Sierra Nevada de Santa Marta, Magdalena.

It is not surprising that the author of the first truly moving love story in Colombian culture should also have been a man who was deeply concerned about our origins and lovingly engaged in the discovery and vindication of the human face of the indigenous cultures that had been erased from our awareness by a mestizo culture that was ashamed of itself.

It is important to note that our culture does not abound in love stories. If there is something that history denied us, it was the festive record of the loves which gave rise to our community. Why do we regard one another as strangers, if it is not that we fail to be the children of a love that unites us?

This question of love and its ways is one of the great and fundamental ones of Colombian history and it also lies at the heart of reflections on the savagery of our wars. In order for opposing armies to regard each other with admiration and respect, like those of the *Iliad*, a fundamental human identification needs to exist, one that overrides family differences, tribal hatreds, scorns of caste and territorial distance. They need to be the offspring of the same gods, with a common descent from some mythical romances. It is not surprising that the author of the first truly moving love story in Colombian culture should also have been a man who was deeply concerned about our origins and lovingly engaged in the discovery and vindication of the human face of the indigenous cultures that had been erased from our awareness by a mestizo culture that was ashamed of itself. At the end of the 19th century, the novelist, politician, explorer and investigator Jorge Isaacs (whose novel *María* – a story, in the splendid setting of the Valle de Cauca, about the love between two adolescents which ends in tragic death – made the whole continent cry) undertook a journey to the Caribbean coast, to the Sierra Nevada de Santa Marta and the Guajira, to study the languages, customs and mythologies of the indigenous peoples of the upper Magdalena River. In an epoch when the academic study of ethnology and anthropology had barely begun in the world, Isaacs was discovering the hidden peoples of his own country, but these revelations were rejected by the pontiffs of official culture, who only saw remnants of the barbaric past in the Indians and believed that they had to be kept concealed or quickly civilized under the destructive shelter of ecclesiastical communities. The then president of Colombia, Miguel Antonio Caro – a Conservative-party grammarian, poet, Latinist and translator of Virgil, bred in the worship of Rome and the Spanish medieval world and hostile to all modernity – denounced Isaacs as an abominable upholder of the evolutionist theories of Darwin and used his power to block his intellectual enterprise. It is also worth recalling that Isaacs devoted a chapter of his novel *María* to exploring the origins of an African princess, who, after being enslaved, winds up becoming part of the staff of servants in the mansion of the parents of the hero.

It was only in the nineteen-thirties and forties that anthropologists (chiefly Gerardo Reichel-Dolmatoff, an Austrian savant who was stirred by the archaeo-

logical and anthropological wealth of Colombia) began to engage in a systematic study of the native peoples – of their diversity, mythologies and philosophies – an enterprise which led Colombian society to truly discover its own indigenous past for the first time.

Thus, García Márquez is not mistaken when he gets the Arabs and the Indians to reach Macondo at the same time. After the colonial age Colombia had entertained the curious illusion, encouraged by its official ideology and political publicists, of being a homogeneous country – white, Catholic, Hispanic and purebred, in the European style. The Indians were a legend from a remote age, solitary snake oil vendors who only emerged on market days to sell remedies and herbs in the villages, or sinister rustic creatures lost in the depths of the prairies, the fastnesses of the wilderness or the mirages of the deserts. For the rest of Colombia, the diversity of their cultures, the murmur of their myths, the beauty of their ornaments and dress, the complexity of their customs, the strangeness of their languages and profundity of their philosophies are something that only emerged in the past fifty years, so that we are still in the middle of the discovery of America. Literature usually failed to take them into account and they did not appear in poetry again after the epic rhymed chronicle of the Discovery written by Juan De Castellanos in the second half of the 16th century, except in that curious poem by Julio Arboleda, *Gonzalo de Oyón*.

In a similar manner, the sons of Africa inhabited our territory for centuries without the rest of society noticing their mental universe and traditions. They only began to appear in their cultural complexity in the above-mentioned chapter of Isaacs' *María*, in the 19th century; the poems of Candelario Obeso, the poet of Mompox; the persistent and secret dialogue between their rhythmical skill and the musical genres of European origin, which gradually gave rise to the musical wealth of the Colombian littorals – the *cumbias, currulaos, porros, mapalés* and *arrullos* – which incorporated music from the indigenous tradition, of course; and finally, the vigorous creations of recent popular music, like the songs of Joe Arroyo and Jairo Varela. They have also made a showy appearance in the world of sports, with boxers like Rocky Valdez and Kid Pambelé, great soccer players like Freddy Rincón and Faustino Asprilla, and weight-lifters like María Isabel Urrutía, who won a gold medal in the Sydney Olympic Games. In literature too, it was only in the past century that the contributions of the descendants of Africa irrupted into our literature, both through novels that specifically deal with the subject of the clash between the cultural traditions of Whites and Blacks, like García Márquez's *Of love and other demons* and the lively and militantly mulatto oeuvre of Manuel Zapata Olivella, or the poetic dialogue with the cultural orbit of the West undertaken by the offspring of the Pacific, like Helcías Martán Góngora, of Guapi, whose "Declaration of Love" (*Declaración de amor*) forms part of the memory of so many Colombians:

Emberá indigenous woman. Catrú River, Baudó, Chocó.

It was only in the nineteen-thirties and forties that anthropologists (chiefly Gerardo Reichel-Dolmatoff, an Austrian savant who was stirred by the archaeological and anthropological wealth of Colombia) began to engage in a systematic study of the native peoples – of their diversity, mythologies and philosophies – an enterprise which led Colombian society to truly discover its own indigenous past for the first time.

Opposite:
Conservatory
of Music.
Ibagué, Tolima.

Above, left: Festival
of Vallenato.
Valledupar, Cesar.

Above, right :
Conservatory
of Music.
Ibagué, Tolima.

Below, left:
Joropo Festival.
Villavicencio, Meta.

Above, right:
National Band
Contest.
Paipa, Boyacá.

86 San Pacho Fiestas.
    Quibdó, Chocó.

The seaweed and fishes
are witnesses that I wrote
your beloved name in the sand many times.

Witnesses are the moon and fireflies,
which taught me to carve your name
on the blue prow of sailboats.

Witnesses are the seaboard palms,
because on their melodious green trunks
my love carved your initials clearly.

My love knows that amid sighs
I described your beauty on the page
of the gray wings of the seagull high above.

And the southern seas, that were mine,
and the southern islands where my voice
put into port with the ships, in search of you.

You alone on the sea, girl whom I call,
wave for the shipwreck of my kisses,
isle of love, do not know that I love you.

So that you may learn, I tell you,
and make the immense sea my witness!

Pages 88-89:
Barranquilla Carnival.
Atlántico.

Every racial mixture engendered by love has a seed of freedom and its result is joy. This fact allows us to understand the warm sensuality, happy vitality and frankness of the mulatto races of the Caribbean.

    The anomalous reality of Colombia, its capricious history, led to the growth of ruling classes who gave the impression of being European, with very precise notions about Paris and Rome, Madrid and Athens, Cesar and Napoleon, and took a long time to acknowledge that they lived in the equinoctial regions of Colombia, near jungles of anacondas and tropical seas with singing whales. This attitude means that many Colombians are familiar with the Eiffel Tower, the Nile, the Great Lakes or the Coliseum of Rome, but not with the monoliths of San Agustín, nor the "Lost City" of the Taironas, nor the fluvial star of the Orinoco, nor the infinite and oceanic ocarinas of the Tumaco culture. It reflects the persistence of a colonial mental model, which worships what is distant and renowned and disdains what is close as something barbaric, and regards what is our own as a private motive for shame.
    This might have been understandable in colonial times, perhaps. But why does it persist two centuries after Independence, when Colombia has ensured its symbolic

place in the world by virtue of the splendor of its natural setting – celebrated by so many travelers – the magic of its novelists and poets, the strength and originality of its artists, the joy and variety of its music, the wealth of its resources, the talent of its athletes and the legendary boldness of its adventurers?

The most effective work of the Conquest, the long Spanish colony and also the convulsive republican experience was the rupture of local memories and the silencing of traditions. The official ideology which rules in Colombia, which rules the mentality of its leaders and guides the discourse of its major communications media, is still a victim of that pitiful colonial discourse which only looked to the metropolis for its paradigms, which centered its dynamic in the imitation of illustrious models, which always felt itself to be a marginal region of the world, and century after century revolved, like a feverish moon, around the old centers of the globe: the Spanish Crown, the Vatican, the French Revolution, English mercantilism, industrialism and the consumerism of the United States.

As we have said, it was less difficult to recognize the importance of the indigenous past in Mexico and Peru, because those pyramids, those cities in the jungles of Central America, those stone relics of the Andes, were much harder to deny or erase, but also because the quick surrender of the central empires enabled the indigenous majorities of those countries to survive and a numerous native population to subsist in their societies despite the terrible demographic decline suffered in the early days of the Conquest. With these immense communities oral tradition survived in certain places, as did the memory of their origins, which was transmitted from generation to generation, whereas in countries, like Colombia, where the destruction of the past was slower and more persistent, the native communities had to seek refuge in the distant and the inaccessible: in the fogs of the sierra, beyond the horizon; in the fastness of the jungle, hidden by mist and rain. The indigenous past was outlawed, but history was also responsible for perpetuating this early experience through ceaseless ruptures with the past that erased any continuity of historical memory.

Here, the Colony represented a persistent effort that can only be described by awkward neologisms, an effort to de-Americanize, to de-Indianize this reality. The transfer of the European world to our territory was meant to be thorough, even though it was known, beforehand, to be impossible. And strange flowers began to appear on this graft between the visible and triumphant, and the secret and defeated. Further on we shall see how the *mestizaje* of different forms of art later acquired the exuberant appearance of Baroque styles. But once again, at the beginning of the 19th century, as has been discerningly pointed out by the historian Hermes Tovar, a vast upheaval, the epic of Independence, led the Republic to be founded on the abstract principles of the French Revolution and the Enlightenment, but strangled the memory of our immediate Hispanic past and even cut the threads that linked us to that tradition. Still later, throughout the 19th century and into the beginning of the 20th, the civil

In a similar manner, the sons of Africa inhabited our territory for centuries without the rest of society noticing their mental universe and traditions. They only began to appear in their cultural complexity in the above-mentioned chapter of Isaacs' María, *in the 19th century; the poems of Candelario Obeso, the poet of Mompox; the persistent and secret dialogue between their rhythmical skill and the musical genres of European origin, which gradually gave rise to the musical wealth of the Colombian littorals –* the cumbias, currulaos, porros, mapalés *and* arrullos *– which incorporated music from the indigenous tradition, of course; and finally, the vigorous creations of recent popular music, like the songs of Joe Arroyo and Jairo Varela.*

Leopoldo Richter. *Black girl of the Pacific coast, drawn for Gisella* (detail), watercolor, 1953. 26.5 x 22 cm.

Pages 92-93: Guillermo Wiedemann. Oil on wood (detail), 1947. 49 x 77 cm.

The country has suddenly shown itself to have a much more diverse geography and much more complex ethnic composition than we thought, and to be much richer in cultures than what we had been taught by tradition. And every Colombian, with the scraps of the old version of the country which he got from his family and school, remains astonished today by a land that surprises him, by the presence of compatriots whom he does not know, by a number of cultural expressions that he never winds up feeling are his own as he tries to protect his awareness of himself by refusing to identify with the joys and sorrows of his fellow citizens.

wars between the Liberals and Conservatives forced countless Colombians into exile and abandonment and cut the links of their memory, their rootedness in the land and their awareness of their origins. But perhaps none of these wars between the Liberals and Conservatives was so effective in causing expulsion and uprooting as the savage violence of the 1950's, which drove millions of persons from their lands, made the cities grow in an unprecedented way and once again hacked down the memory of origins and the voice of tradition. And, tinged with a discourse about a supposed modernization that pretended that the urban was not a compulsory punishment but the ideal of modernity, abruptly turned our rustic cities into great metropolises riven by discrimination and isolation. In a country of mountains, it converted the word *montañero* (highlander) into an offensive insult and once more made whole communities, those from the central part of the country, the most densely populated of all, victims of this forgetfulness of the recent past.

Such has been the process that made Colombia perhaps the most forgetful country of the continent: one of the least aware of its historical past and even its recent experiences. For centuries the Blacks and Mulattoes slumbered on its shores, distant from its history; the only reference point for the Mestizos of the mountains was their immediate past as peasant-farmers. That rural country completely forgot that its forefathers had been explorers and navigators on a global scale.

Confinement in Andean villages and in ports closed off from the world sent the country into a long sleep, without the slightest contact with the outside world. Or only one: the Catholic Church, which ruled their lives from distant Rome. An initial attempt to encourage immigration in the 19th century ran up against the resistance of the potential immigrants from Europe, who preferred the northern or southern parts of the Americas, because their climates were more familiar. Later on, official policy preferred to hinder immigration, and thus there came into being that curious racial type, the Colombian, the fruit of a mixture between the diverse races of Spain and the equally diverse indigenous and African ones, with very few immigrants from other regions.

But, by driving the masses of Colombia from their plots of land to the growing cities, it was the violence of the 1950's that confronted every Colombian with the complexity of a country of which he was almost completely unaware, a country of which he had only been given an impoverished version at school, learned from primers in which the animals were wolves and nightingales and the fruits apples and grapes. The country has suddenly shown itself to have a much more diverse geography and much more complex ethnic composition than we thought, and to be much richer in cultures than what we had been taught by tradition.

Opposite: Weaver of hammocks. San Jacinto, Bolívar.

Page 96: A *taita* (shaman) of the Inga indigenous group, resting in his hammock at dawn. Putumayo.

Page 97: *Grammar of the Chibcha language.* Historical archive of Colegio Mayor de Nuestra Señora del Rosario. Bogotá.

96 *The most effective work of the Conquest, the long Spanish colony and also the convulsive republican experience was the rupture of local memories and the silencing of traditions. The official ideology which rules in Colombia, which rules the mentality of its leaders and guides the discourse of its major communications media, is still a victim of that pitiful colonial discourse which only looked to the metropolis for its paradigms, which centered its dynamic in the imitation of illustrious models, which always felt itself to be a marginal region of the world, and century after century revolved, like a feverish moon, around the old centers of the globe: the Spanish Crown, the Vatican, the French Revolution…*

GRAMATICA EN LA LENGVA GENERAL DEL NVEVO REYNO, LLAMADA MOSCA.

Compuesto por el Padre Fray Bernardo de Lugo, Predicador General del Orden de Predicadores, y Catedratico de la dicha lengua, en el Conuento del Rosario de la ciudad de Santa Fe.

Año 1619.

En Madrid, por Barnardino de Guzmã

THE LESSONS LEFT BY POETRY

One of the most harmful practices in the history of Colombia, which survived much longer here than in other countries, was the formal censorship of books by the Church, which wrongfully turned into the guardian of the State and protagonist of political life. The Catholic Index prohibited the freedom to read until well into the 20th century and, unfortunately, the levels of reading are still very low in Colombia compared to countries like Argentina or Mexico, not to speak of the countries of Europe to which Colombia may be compared by virtue of its size and population.

Once we had abandoned our oral memory, the books which would have replaced it in Europe never arrived. Once the dependence on Spain was broken, we set out to forget the ties that united our peoples with the peninsula that had given us our blood and tongue. It is a difficult and thrilling subject for historians, this problem of not only reconstructing the past, but also finding out why and how our remote past seemed be erased from the memory of our communities: why our historical memory did not come to be a fundamental part of our personal and collective life; how we fell into the tendency to also forget the recent past, to not inherit the experience accumulated over generations; how we became accustomed to living by improvisation and in the moment.

Experiences like the Medellín International Poetry Festival, where thousands of persons attend the recitals of poets from all over the world, reveal the persistence in some regions of an intense longing for oral memory. It is likewise evident in the thrilling pedagogical labor of investigators of oral literature like Estanislao Zuleta and the persistent quest in Antioquia for a literary language that is capable of capturing the secrets of popular speech – its liveliness and devilry – as seen in the works of Efe Gómez, Tomás Carrasquilla, Manuel Mejía Vallejo and Fernando Vallejo.

This may be explained by the fact that we partly belong to the indigenous world, but it has also do with the weak impact of written memory, the alternative for a culture of readers, on our society, even though the Independence was inspired by the thought of the French Revolution and the preceding Enlightenment. The precarious democracy that was born with the republic was stained by slavery, but also by the conviction of its Creole leaders, now in power, that the rest of the population was an inferior species of mankind and did not merit the benefits of culture and prosperity. Night and day, racial, cultural and geographical prejudices worked on the hearts of those arrogant Creoles, who were determined, not to exalt the people, but replace their former peninsular rulers, to the point where they adopted an attitude that was even more discriminatory than that which the latter were ever able to show.

It was even understandable why the Creole domination wound up being more hateful: when all was said and done, they were also mestizos, resembling the mestizo and mulatto masses a little more than they did the Spanish. Thus it was necessary to carry their haughtiness to an extreme and strengthen the differences, so that they would not be confused with those plebeians whom they hated and be able to maintain the

Opposite: Incunabula, books printed before the year 1500. Historical archive of Colegio Mayor de Nuestra Señora del Rosario. Bogotá.

Pages 100-101: Pedro A. Quijano. *The Founding of Bogotá* (detail), oil. 1938. Academia de Historia. Bogotá.

Luis Fonseca. *Pietro Crespi reading while Amaranta embroiders* (detail), 1970, acrylic on canvas. 59.5 x 49.5 cm. Banco de la República.

Right up to the mid-20th century, Colombia, which took pride in calling its capital the Athens of South America, remained wreathed in a medieval fog of priests and party bosses, while most of its neighboring countries had embraced some of the basic advantages of Western modernity.

laughable illusion of being the masters by virtue of their higher rank. The inspiration of the French Revolution posed the challenge of democracy: establishing a minimum equality before the law. This, in turn, should have required the formation of citizens who were modern, educated, well-informed, critical and exigent. But in the eyes of those Creole lords, if servants become educated, they are no longer willing to remain servants. If they become well-informed, they begin to meddle with things that are not their concern. If they assume a critical attitude towards social questions, things become uncomfortable and embarrassing. And if they begin to make demands, they will soon believe that they have the right to be the masters of something.

It is not that the State had accidentally forgotten that education was important or that it did not have sufficient resources to carry out the educational revolution that so many centuries of oppression and exclusion required if it were to form true citizens. For the ruling class, failing to educate, in the noble sense of forming citizens, was and continued to be a priority. It was only grudgingly that they resigned themselves to providing the information and training needed to form good operatives and productive overseers. Even today, when the subject of education arises, the technocrats usually think that the solution is not to effect a major renovation of its guiding philosophy and long-term strategy, but to design rapid methods of training to produce instant factory hands and technicians with basic skills.

They never regard the potential learners as sensitive human beings who deserve to be treated with dignity, but only see them as demographical factors that need a minimum training. They forget that, if they do not receive a worthwhile education as citizens and human beings, even the poorest factory hands may be more dangerous than Tamerlane's hordes. They forget that failing to invest in education is automatically the same as investing in ignorance, fanaticism, resentment and social inequality, and that the victims of this educational negligence are not only the poor but the whole of society, including its most powerful and best educated members.

One of the most harmful practices in the history of Colombia, which survived much longer here than in other countries, was the formal censorship of books by the Church, which wrongfully turned into the guardian of the State and protagonist of political life. The Catholic Index prohibited the freedom to read until well into the 20th century and, unfortunately, the levels of reading are still very low in Colombia compared to countries like Argentina or Mexico, not to speak of the countries of Europe to which Colombia may be compared by virtue of its size and population. If we need to come up with other differences that explain why things happen in Colombia that do not happen in Mexico or Ecuador or Argentina or Venezuela, it is sufficient to recall that the separation of Church and State, agrarian reform and the establishment of lay education are tasks that began in Mexico with the late-19th century Reform and were strengthened by the Revolution. The same kind of reforms were carried out in Argentina during the governments of Roca

104 Maillart. *The mount of Agony*, drawing. From the book: *L'Amérique Equinoxiale*. M. E. André. París, 1879.

Opposite, above: *Slaves working*, 19th century. From the book: *Viajes pintorescos a las dos Américas*.

Opposite, below: *Dinner in a wealthy home, Santa Marta*, 19th century. From the book: *Viajes pintorescos a las dos Américas*.

Such has been the continual process of rupture that made Colombia perhaps the most forgetful country of the continent: one of the least aware of its historical past and even its recent experiences. For centuries the Blacks and Mulattoes slumbered on its shores, distant from its history; the only reference point for the Mestizos of the mountains was the immediate past of their villages. That rural country completely forgot that its forefathers had been adventurers, explorers and navigators on a global scale and a vast region of small farmers scattered throughout the mountains of Antioquia and Santander lost any notion of their origins and began to think that history had begun with them.

105

Opposite: El Tunal Public Library. Bogotá.

Pages 108-109: Luis Ángel Arango Library. Bogotá.

It is not that the State had accidentally forgotten that education was important or that it did not have sufficient resources to carry out the educational revolution that so many centuries of oppression and exclusion required if it were to form true citizens. For the ruling class, failing to educate, in the noble sense of forming citizens, was and continued to be a priority. It was only grudgingly that they resigned themselves to providing the information and training needed to form good operatives and productive overseers.

and Irigoyen at the beginning of the 20th century and in Ecuador by the work of Eloy Alfaro in the same period.

Right up to the mid-20th century, Colombia, which took pride in calling its capital the Athens of South America, remained wreathed in a medieval fog of priests and party bosses, while most of its neighboring countries had embraced some of the basic advantages of Western modernity. A solid proof of it is that when Colombians wanted to get married in a civil ceremony, they were forced to go to any of the neighboring countries, traveling to Venezuela, Ecuador or Panama to be able to enjoy one of the most elementary privileges of modern democracy: even the officials that upheld the clerical State made use of this trick when they had to. Nevertheless, as the philosopher Danilo Cruz Veléz rightly points out, from the very beginning literature had been the true gauge of the country. Colombian literature is very rich and as early as the Conquest it had seen the arrival of the infinite epic of Juan de Castellanos. To deal with reality in literature only seems possible after a long tradition has elapsed: in the beginning it is easier to fantasize and create ideal and mythical worlds as a refuge for the imagination. That is why it is so important to remember the strange voice of Castellanos, the earliest Colombian poet and, it might be said, the first Colombian of which we are aware, in the noble sense that Bolívar would have used that demanding word. In fact, the word "Colombian" only seems fitting when the person whom it describes belongs to modernity, to the epoch which unfolded from the encounter of the two worlds: it implies not failing to recognize the profoundly European nature of its culture, but, at the same time, acknowledging the vast tacit body of America which gives that name its historical significance and transcendence.

Juan de Castellanos, an Andalusian, arrived at the continent at an early age. He was 22 years old when he saw the pearl fisheries of the Cabo de la Vela, in what is now the Colombian department of la Guajira, and from then onwards his life was closely linked to the destiny of Colombia, both the Colombia which exists today and the broad notion of Colombia that Bolívar proposed. The Bard of the Discovery, Castellanos is the founder of the poetic tradition of at least seven countries: he sang about the invasion of Puerto Rico by Juan Ponce de León and his troops, Alvardo's invasion of Cuba, Garay's of the island of Jamaica and that of Ortal and Sedeño on the island of Trinidad; the conquest of Hispaniola, the long and painful conquest of Venezuela by the German captains Georgio Spira, Nicolás de Federmán, Ambrosio Alfínger and Felipe de Hutten; the conquest of the Kingdom of Santa Marta, the Guajira and the Sierra Nevada; the conquest of the Sinú and the founding of Cartagena by Pedro de Heredia; the conquest of the River Magdalena and the New Kingdom of Granada, from the land of Yuldama in Honda to the peaks of the Central Cordillera, by way of the slopes of the Guarinó, by Gonzalo Jiménez de Quesada; the founding of Pasto, Popayán and Cali by Sebastián de Belalcázar; the conquest of Antioquia and the discovery of the Chocó. Castellanos even managed to chant

de Orellana's journey through the Amazon in 1541, the bloody voyage of Pedro de Ursúa and his murderer Lope de Aguirre twenty years later and the first assaults by English pirates on the fortresses of the Caribbean.

Whoever wants to find the earliest fresco of Colombia, the earliest full-scale picture, violent and excessive but harmonious and loving as well, of what would come to be called Colombia in the course of the centuries, only has to read the royal octets of Juan de Castellanos, which are as copious and meticulous as a great adventure novel, but also rich in melodious verses and in curious and poignant human details.

One of the many lessons left us by those *Elegías de varones ilustres de Indias* (Elegies of illustrious men of the Indies) is to see the way in which some of the Spanish conquistadors were bearers of a high culture, of an education that was broad and profound at the same time. The manner in which Castellanos shows his familiarity with the Greek and Latin classics, Arabic learning and the savants of his time is overwhelming. It is surprising to discover that a society which came to be so provincial in later epochs was founded on such solid cultural references, on such a universal curiosity, on a language so rich, so sophisticated and so full of resources.

Opposite: Nazareth, La Guajira.

Abajo: Procession of the Nazarene, Easter Week. Mompox, Bolívar.

Pages 112-113: Easter Week. Pamplona, Santander del Norte.

The word "Colombian" only seems fitting when the person whom it describes belongs to modernity, to the epoch which unfolded from the encounter of the two worlds: it implies not failing to recognize the profoundly European nature of its culture, but, at the same time, acknowledging the vast tacit body of America which gives that name its historical significance and transcendence.

A COUNTRY OF CONTRASTS

But the Colony carried out its work in our land in a manner that was effective and mysterious at the same time. If, in the 16th century, poetry was dazzled by the territory of America, with its caimans and snakes, its *chigüiros* (capybaras, the largest living rodent.) and tapirs, its enormous *ceiba* and *caimito* trees, its thatched huts and hurricanes; by the diversity of indigenous nations with gold ornaments and diadems of colored feathers; by the highly detailed reality of war and the clash of two worlds, but also by the dense matter of the millenary world of America, the following centuries seemed to lose that sense of bewilderment, that amplitude of gaze, that capacity to see the two worlds and celebrate their embrace, so that poetry and art began to reflect the now triumphant mother country and wished to live its adventures as though America did not exist or was not allowed to exist. The very disorder of the Conquest had brought an immense freedom to the spirit of the adventurers, but now the abiding triumph of the Crown and Church acted as a powerful check on the creativity of artists. Nevertheless, it is not true to say that America would never emerge in colonial literature and art, it is just that it began to emerge in a disguised form, cloaked by the outward appearances of the illustrious world that triumphed over it. There thus arrived the epoch of veiled fusions and hermetic languages, the epoch in which the profuse material of America began to be reinterpreted in a Western Baroque style.

In the work of Hernando Domínguez Camargo – the great rival of Góngora – or Álvarez de Velasco y Zorilla; in the carvings of Legarda that adorned the altars of the churches of Quito and Popayán; in the decorations of fruits and flowers in the chapels of Tunja; in the bicephalous eagles of precious stones and the dazzling green circles of the monstrances of emeralds, what we call the Baroque from then onwards becomes, at times, a normal expression of that exuberance, already mentioned, that characterizes our natural setting, and at other times, a poor European interpretation of the complexities of the American world.

In Europe to be classical means that a work resembles the austere and gentle aspects of nature; in our tropics nature is a synonym for extravagance and excess. We might say that an apple or a bunch of grapes, a nightingale or deer, are the emblematic forms of the European classical world, but from that perspective, a pineapple or other fruits like the *guanábana* or *pitahaya,* or a bunch of the palm nuts known as *chontaduro,* or a caiman or an armadillo, may suggest Baroque forms. All of our natural world, with

Bat-man. Tairona pectoral. Gold Museum, Banco de la República. Bogotá.

In Europe to be classical means that a work resembles the austere and gentle aspects of nature; in our tropics nature is a synonym for extravagance and excess.

116 San Ignacio Church. Bogotá.

Opposite: San Agustín Church. Bogotá.

It is possible that much of what we call American Baroque also represented the free irruption of the native sensibility and profusion of tropical forms into Mestizo America and the lands not so closely controlled by the Spanish.

Below, left: *Siiria*, sash woven in cotton threads, Guajiro indigenous culture.

Below, right: Cuna necklaces.

Opposite, left: Arhauco *mochila* (woven shoulder bag).

Opposite, right: Cuna *mola* (fabric with patchwork design).

the native cultures at its heart, would have seemed like a mosaic of fantastic shapes to sensitive observers: the painted bodies of the Emberá, half day, half night; the infinite necklaces of the Cuna; the fabrics with patchwork designs known as molas, whose contrasting colors transmit the electric energy of nature; faces scored with achiote dye; the bright blue skirts of the Guambianos; the black and white geometry of the Arhuaco *mochilas* (woven shoulder bags); the infinite number of stone slabs of the lost cities of the Sierra Nevada de Santa Marta; the green plumage of the *guadua* bamboo groves that follow water courses; the *platanillo* flowers which look like motionless flocks of fire; the prairies of purple heliconia which stand like ceremonial staffs; macaws, strident to the ear and eye; beaches pink with flamingos; white trees weighed down by herons at dusk; highways that smell of mangoes; toucans with enormous beaks; solitary *yarumo* trees, silver in the darkness of the forest and woody *sietecueros* with purple flowers; armored armadillos; branches on which all the colors of the rainbow sing; the colored walls of the equinoctial twilight above the Amazonian rivers.

In Castellanos excess was in the background, in the very material he dealt with: in the finery of the warriors of Trinidad, who wore jaguar's teeth mounted in gold, and used the sharp teeth of sharks and stings of rays as arrow points, worked with exquisite art to bestow the silent death of which Wordsworth spoke. From then on, the forms, verbal resources and ornaments also became messengers of that wealth, even against

a background of rigid European messages. From then on, profusion, as an insignia of art, would never forsake us, although one of the facets of that abundance might have been, precisely, austerity.

The regional fiestas of Colombia have always been joyfully ruled by that apparel of excess and that law of contrasts. You see it in the Carnival of Barranquilla, which fills the streets with human animals, which deploys every imaginable color in the vitality of its endless dances; in the beauty contest in Cartagena, where it is possible to see the young queens in a fancy dress that is overwhelmed by extravagant jewelry and immense feathers which are vaguely inspired by birds and ancient indigenous processions; in the "Devil's Carnival" of Riosucio, a fusion of native and African rites in the heart of the white, Catholic culture of the mountains.

Nevertheless, it is surprising to find in Carlyle's *Sartor Resartus*, that kind of world history of clothing, that when the philosopher tries to describe the most austere dress that mankind has ever invented, he does not choose the *chlamys* of Ancient Greece (a cloak doubled or pinned over one shoulder) or Roman toga or Gypsy *pareo* (wrap dress) or African cloaks, but the single garment worn over the shoulders by the ragged and practically naked soldiers of the Liberator Simón Bolívar in the mortally cold high moors of the Andes: a square of cloth with a straight slit in the center. Thus it was that, in Carlyle's book, the abstract idea of the poncho and its Colombian equivalent,

All of our natural world, with the native cultures at its heart, would have seemed like a mosaic of fantastic shapes to sensitive observers: the painted bodies of the Emberá, half day, half night; the infinite necklaces of the Cuna; the embroidered fabrics known as molas, *whose contrasting colors transmit the electric energy of nature; faces scored with achiote dye; the bright blue skirts of the Guambianos; the black and white geometry of the Arhuaco* mochilas *(woven shoulder bags)…*

120

Above: International Theater Festival. Bogotá.

Below: National Band Festival. Paipa, Boyacá.

Opposite, above: Festival of the Bambuco. Neiva, Huila.

Opposite, below: Carnival of the Whites and Blacks. Pasto, Nariño.

The regional fiestas of Colombia have always been joyfully ruled by that apparel of excess and that law of contrasts. You see it in the Carnival of Barranquilla, which fills the streets with human animals, which deploys every imaginable color in the vitality of its endless dances; in the beauty contest in Cartagena, where it is possible to see the young queens in a fancy dress that is overwhelmed by extravagant jewelry and immense feathers which are vaguely inspired by birds and ancient indigenous processions; in the "Devil's Carnival" of Riosucio, a fusion of native and African rites in the heart of the white, Catholic culture of the mountains.

122 Carnival of Barranquilla. Atlántico.

the *ruana*, possibly owed to the refined sense of design of the continent's Indians, won the honor of being declared the greatest example of sobriety in human dress.

After Juan de Castellanos, the great literary works of Colombia seemed to lose interest in the American world and seek refuge in an ostentatious re-elaboration of the European world and the mental universe of Catholicism. Spain had triumphed and it looked as though its transplantation to the tropics had been achieved without major obstacles by then. But when we look at the work of Hernando Domínguez Camargo, we are confronted, once again, by a number of aesthetic proposals that do not easily fit into the canons. The heroic poem in honor of St. Ignatius of Loyola, written by this Creole Jesuit in the 17th century, is a curious example of *culteranismo*, a precious, latinized, highly metaphorical style of that period, and has often been criticized for its excess, daring use of metaphor and lack of proportion. It is, to take the term to an extreme, a kind of excessive Baroque. But once again we find in it something that was typical of the epochs in which Europe was implanting itself in America.

There was not a single field of reality in which this transplanting was effected without a fight. And what tended, for an ingenuous or ordinary gaze, to manifest itself as imperfection was often the irruption of more complex problems into the process of forging works of art. If our artists had restricted themselves to copying, everything might have been much easier and their works would have been accepted without reservation. But no true artist is capable of such renunciation: his concern is creation and every creation is a dialogue between memory and the present, between the established languages and new resources, between mankind and the individual.

In European Baroque you feel the will towards image, the imperative of representation, as Marcello Fagiolo wrote in *The great theater of the baroque*. It is a magnification of the effort to make the world exclusively human, where everything that the eye may see is elaborated, controlled, by a human contortion and, you might even say, by a sensual emphasis: the effort, stimulated by the Council of Trent, to reveal the spirit in every form of physical reality.

The world of the artist stopped being the world and turned into the soul. In the end, it was this long process of the humanization of the natural that would enable Byron to say, in his poetry, that even the mountains were sentiment and allow Romanticism to make nature reflect all human emotions. One of the aims of European Baroque was to turn the world into a theater and, in the specific case of the Church, to exalt its temples into theaters that would allow humans to experience a foretaste of the splendors of Heaven. Thus architecture became a "stage setting device", of which the baldachin of St. Peter's in Rome would be the extreme example.

But in the 16th century, a renewed fascination with gold swept over Europe, a wish to convert gold into atmosphere, into the celestial vault, and to fill the horizon with that luxurious twilight. The gold of America had irrupted into its awareness, the gold of the Aztecs and Incas and later the gold of Nueva Granada. From that time onwards

We must remind ourselves, over and over again, that our countries are inconceivable without modernity and contact with the rest of the world. In current times, there are very few communities which may claim the privilege of belonging to a tradition that is self-enclosed, the master of its own, exclusive cosmogony, language, philosophy, system of myths, dress, ornamental style, medicine, ancestral space and magical universe. It is true, of course, that present-day Colombia has some of these communities among its components, full of cultural treasures, deeply rooted in a territory over centuries, possessors of a wisdom that will be surely be vital for our future, for it holds some of the clues to the survival of our planet.

124 Above, left: Carnival of Barranquilla. Atlántico.

Above, right: The *Cuadrillas* of San Martín. Meta.

Below, left: The "Devil's Carnival". Riosucio, Caldas.

Below, right: Easter Week. Popayán, Cauca.

Carnival of Barranquilla. Atlántico.

... escaping from restraint has always been a Latin American recourse and is the equivalent of the strongest form of resistance, refusing to let a European kind of humanism exert its tyranny over a natural universe that surpasses it. Auden maintained that nothing in America inspires us to regard nature as though it were a human mother, that the gods have another countenance here.

Santa Clara Church. Bogotá.

But in the 16th century, a renewed fascination with gold swept over Europe, a wish to convert gold into atmosphere, into the celestial vault, and to fill the horizon with that luxurious twilight. The gold of America had irrupted into its awareness, the gold of the Aztecs and Incas and later the gold of Nueva Granada. From that time onwards the golden grotto, one of the earliest characteristically Latin American symbolic spaces, led to a kind of shifting of the myth of Eldorado to the field of religion: the sparkling vault of the sky was now the mystical womb of Mary, the means by which the Church of Rome entered into dialogue with the gold of America.

the golden grotto, one of the earliest characteristically Latin American symbolic spaces, led to a kind of shifting of the myth of Eldorado to the field of religion: the sparkling vault of the sky was now the mystical womb of Mary, the means by which the Church of Rome entered into dialogue with the gold of America. The critic Damián Bayon maintained that the Baroque, far from being an absolute imposition by authority, was also an invasion of the wild, fantasy-prone European peasant spirit, which entered into the colder, more measured, better organized and classical culture of the cities. It is possible that much of what we call American Baroque also represented the free irruption of the native sensibility and profusion of tropical forms into Mestizo America and the lands not so closely controlled by the Spanish. We might say that in literature and poetry the broad and diverse languages that we call Baroque here arise, instead, as a popular endeavor to interpret the world by going beyond a set of merely human canons. In it the abstract spirit of indigenous painting – the refusal to utilize a figurative realism, the survival of animism, of the sacred sense of nature as it is conceived in the indigenous myths – prevented too full a triumph of the classical canon. From then onwards, the Mestizo arts were our own and we always see in them a kind of victory of the grotesque over the stereotyped and symmetrically harmonious forms of humanist art: a victory of the vital unruliness of nature, of the electric brush strokes and vigorous color contrasts.

In aesthetics there is always a battle between form and content: classicisms imprison form, expressionisms destroy it. The adventure of the English Pre-Raphaelites was a self-contradictory attempt to free themselves from the parameters which classical art had imposed on reality, but without daring to break with form. In Góngora, a typical Andalusian influenced by the presence of the Arab world, it is possible to note an attempt to let the music of his verses ride away with their meaning, and this produces an effect of disorder. In the same way, escaping from restraint has always been a Latin American recourse and is the equivalent of the strongest form of resistance, refusing to let a European kind of humanism exert its tyranny over a natural universe that surpasses it. Auden maintained that nothing in America inspires us to regard nature as though it were a human mother, that the gods have another countenance here.

In fact, what most resembles divinity as this America might conceive of it are works like the awesome novel by José Eustasio Rivera, *La vorágine* (The Vortex); the jaguar in Borges' *La escritura del Dios* ("The scripture of God", a story in which a pre-Columbian magician, imprisoned by the Spaniards, learns to read the markings on a tiger); the multiple god of the pantheists which is man in mankind and ant in the ant kingdom or the highly-elaborate idea of the cosmic serpent found in the mythologies of the inhabitants of the Amazon, whose mythical nature is sub-aquatic and arboreal at the same time, and sidereal in that its skin is a map of the constellations. It is thus worth reading Domínguez Camargo as a dialogue between the European religious spirit and the American worlds, between the forms which try to enclose the world and the contents that do not let themselves be trapped:

128 Popular religious art. Boyacá.

Opposite: Zona Rosa, the district of fashionable restaurants, bars, boutiques and discos. Bogotá.

From then onwards, the Mestizo arts were our own and we always see in them a kind of victory of the grotesque over the stereotyped and symmetrically harmonious forms of humanist art: a victory of the vital unruliness of nature, of the electric brush strokes and vigorous color contrasts.

> In she who drinks, there is thirst the more she drinks;
> in she who eats there is unsatisfied hunger,
> when she most feels pleasure; in she who
> compresses into a brief moment an eternity of pleasure;
> in she in whom the soul moves in sweet peace
> through spheres of enraptured love,
> and is a sea of thirst, a sweet lethargy,
> an ocean of hunger, an abyss of beauty…

It is worth tracking down these variations on the theme of excess, from the excessive and powerful verses of the *Poema heroico a san Ignacio de Loyola* to the twists and turns of *La vorágine*. It is worth tracking them down, from the plays on words of Álvarez de Velasco y Zorrilla to the extravagant verbal fireworks of León de Greiff:

> I have not seen the sea,
> My eyes
> – sharp-sighted watchmen, fantastic fireflies –
> my eyes alert amidst the night, owners
> of the starry camber,
> of the astral worlds,
> my roving eyes, my pensive eyes,
> my eyes have not seen the sea,
> I have not seen the sea.
>
> The undulating canticle of your tremulous curve
> has not rocked my dreams,
> nor did I hear the erotic moaning of your sirens,
> nor was my retina dazed with the resplendent quicksilver
> that rolls off your back…

It is a whole adventure to perceive this profusion, which runs from the dazzling and bloodstained Caribbean of Juan de Castellanos to the intricate family tree of the races of Gabriel García Márquez, and to see the way how European art is sent back to Europe in the form of the agonized voluptuousness of Luis Caballero's painting, or those placid colored postcards, spilling over with irony: the tropical pictures painted by Fernando Botero, drunk with excess and at the same time marvelously restrained and still and bathed in a Renaissance luminosity.

Store selling religious statues. 20 de Julio district. Bogotá

Every time that we ask ourselves who we are and what Colombia is, we must examine those complex origins, evident in a number of highly visible elements and symbols: the Spanish language enriched by the American experience; the religion of Christ highly tinged by our triple indigenous, European and African universe…

Above, left: *San Marcos* (St. Mark) 17th century, high relief in polychrome wood, with gilded details. Pulpit of Santa Clara Church. Bogotá.

Above, right: *San Antonio de Padua* (St. Anthony of Padua), taller neogranadino (School of Nueva Granada), 18th century, mezzo relievo on wood. Museum of Colonial Art. Bogotá.

Below, left: *Canephora*, taller boyacense (School of Boyacá), 18th century, carved polychrome wood. Museum of Colonial Art. Bogotá.

Below, right: *Sacred Heart of Jesus*, Museum of Colonial Art. Bogotá.

Eucharistic Christ (detail), Figueroa studio, oil on canvas. 192 x 124 cm.

Pages 134-135: Luis Caballero, *Anecdotal painting, triptych* (detail), 1973, oil on paper. 195 x 390 cm.

One of the aims of European Baroque was to turn the world into a theater and, in the specific case of the Church, to exalt its temples into theaters that would allow humans to experience a foretaste of the splendors of Heaven. Thus architecture became a "stage setting device", of which the baldachin of St. Peter's in Rome would be the extreme example.

A JOURNEY THROUGH COLOMBIA

How can you be methodical in a land where nature has the curious characteristic of ceaselessly mixing everything up with everything else? In every square meter, how many different species of plants ! At every few kilometers, another climate! Variety imposes itself on you when you do the most ordinary journey, through any part of the country. Let's take, for example, the journey by land between Bogotá and Cali, the same one that was done by so many Indians on foot, so many conquistadors on horseback, so many astonished foreign travelers over the centuries. The meticulous journey of Baron von Humboldt: from the central high plains to the west, descending to the valley of the River Magdalena; climbing again, over the Central Cordillera, to the its high point, La Línea; and then descending to the Western Cordillera, beyond whose stony outcrops is hidden the ocean . You might say that in this five hundred kilometer-long trip, at the speed and on the roads that one travels today, we see all the climates, all the trees, all the topographies of the country.

The journey commences on the savanna of Bogotá, the cold prairie that lies 2,600 meters above sea level, where today there stretches a jumbled metropolis of eight million inhabitants in the shadow of the eastern mountain ridges; a savanna that was formed by the drying up of an enormous lake encircled by mountains that emerged in the Cretaceous period. This fertile Andean high plain was sown with maize plantations in the times of the great kingdom of the Muiscas and lies close to the high paramos (Andean moors) of the Sumapaz, silent regions covered by wooly *frailejón* plants and *chusque* bamboos, a dense vegetation that is blotted out by the mist. Here, in the late 19th century, when this vast, densely vegetated plain still spread around a village of pious belfries, one of the founding poets of Latin American modernism, José Asunción Silva, sang of his misfortunes in melodious verses which, as Jorge Luis Borges says, America has not been willing to forget. In one of his poems, his summoned up for us the most magical night of the continent:

> One night,
> one night all full of perfumes, murmurs and the music of wings.
> One night,
> in which there glowed, in the humid nuptial shadow,
> the fantastic fireflies,
> by my side, slowly, wholly encircled by me,

Opposite: El Tolima snow-covered mountain. Tolima.

Pages 138-139: Procession of the silleteros (chair-carriers). Flower Festival. Medellín, Antioquia.

What we now call Colombia (because there were other Colombias in the past and there will probably be others, different to it, in the future) is a challenge for those who think that a nation is defined by its oneness.

> silent and pale,
> as though a premonition of infinite bitterness
> disturbed you to the most secret depth of your fibers,
> along the path that crosses the flowering plain,
> you walked…

Opposite: Darién jungle. Chocó.

Pages 142-143: Plaza de Bolívar. Primatial Cathedral in background. Bogotá.

You have only to travel round any region to feel the splendor of nature in Colombia: its dense, bio-diverse jungles in the south and west, the sea of trees in the Amazon, the rain forests of the Pacific; the mist forests in the three cordilleras into which the Andes divide before pooling into the prairies of the Caribbean…

Leaving the savanna which, then, amidst acacias and yellow-flowered *alcaparros* (caper trees), fills with black araucaria pines and high and fragile *urapanes*, the traveler reaches the edge of those dark cliffs which open out towards the valley of the Magdalena, from which slope down great, aromatic forests of eucalyptus with dappled trunks and blue leaves. It is a stirring moment when there unfold the countless mountains where green is of all colors, the nearest ones yellow-, ivy- and moss-green and further on, across the endless peaks, greens that are ever more blue, barely contrasted by patches of mist.

Less an hour has passed and we are already crossing the flowery slopes of a warmer climate, as we descend from Fusa to Chinauta and see the sweeping panoramas of a region of slanting planes formed millions of years ago by the melting of great icecaps on the summits above the Sumapaz River. From there we descend amidst phosphorescent bougainvillea , steep walls and vertiginous, unstable rocky abysses that fall down towards the hotlands, and lead us to the canyons of el Boquerón, where the equinoctial light seems to scratch symmetrical wounds on the rock walls high above. The atmosphere, which had already grown warm as we descended to the canyon, where stone gorges stretch out along the river, is full of moist boiling air by the time we pass beneath the huge rock, known as the "Devil's Nose", that projects over the highway through a landscape that makes one think of the remote time of uproar, many millennia ago, when the waters opened the canyon with a catastrophic force. Now the heat is only the prelude for the equatorial tulips with their enormous red flowers. Here, you almost here the ancestral voice of Jorge Isaacs, declaiming his most beautiful verse:

> I dreamt of wandering through groves of palm trees…

Palms fill the mountain flank and the wooded plain that leads us to Melgar and Girardot, to the banks of the brown waters of the River Magdalena. It is impossible to describe the variety of trees there: *ceibas* and *samanes, caracolíes, guamos* and *písamos, gualandayes* and *cámbulos* – trees with thick trunks, trees with immense leaves, and in the midst of the green forest, a *guayacán* in flower like a streak of light. The haciendas are there, the cattle tiny in the high grass, the distant horizon weighed down by the hugeness of the clouds, the plains of el Espinal sown with crops, the heart of Tolima, where clouds of fierce mosquitoes rise at dusk and you see the slow herons, the balsas and the mangoes with their very dense foliage, and the sweeping valley, only watched over by the Colombian vultures, the black *gallinazos* who fly high in the air with a delightful

144 Albert Berg. *El Tolima Volcano* (detail), 1855, oil painting.

Two centuries ago, Humboldt, dazzled by these changing landscapes, went to the north of Tolima to explore the Santa Ana gold mines and, setting off from Ibagué, crossed the cordillera to the Viceroy's house in Cartago. At times, from this middle prairie, and only when nature allows it, the ultra-white cone of the snow-covered Nevado del Tolima reveals itself.

perfection. Finally, another town asleep beneath a cloud of trees, Gualanday, announces the bend where the plain ends, where you clamber up a steep terrain again, passing on the intermediate level defiles with plains of rice fields, flowery *ocobos, gualandayes* and *cámbulo*s, to reach Ibagué, in the shadow of the snow-covered peaks.

Two centuries ago, Humboldt, dazzled by these changing landscapes, went to the north of Tolima to explore the Santa Ana gold mines and, setting off from Ibagué, crossed the cordillera to the Viceroy's house in Cartago. At times, from this middle prairie, and only when nature allows it, the ultra-white cone of the snow-covered Nevado del Tolima reveals itself. Here is the city with its indigenous and mestizo countenances, with its skillful makers of guitars and *tiples* (a small instrument of the guitar family, with 12 strings in 4 sets). But the road seeks the other flank of the cordillera, a winding route that runs beneath woods of *carboneros* with outstretched branches which scale the hillsides and shade the gullies.

It will not take long for the thermal level to change: plantains with enormous leaves appear, each leaf the size of a man, torn by the wind, with clusters of tall flowers, and the River Cocora flowing near Coello, the paradise of the poet Álvaro Mutis, the site of the hot climate farm where he spent his childhood. Here too we may pause for a moment, try to make night fall over the world, and go back a number of decades, if need be, as though there were no noise of cars nor roar of trucks on the highways, but only that Colombian rain, dense and profound, and in it the sleepless voice of a man who returns to this place from his exile every day, who invokes, over and over again, the sublime nights of Tolima, who, in his "Nocturne" celebrates the gift of rain in this very twilight:

> Tonight the rain falls once more on the coffee groves,
> on the leaves of plantain,
> on the high branches of the cámbulos;
> it is raining again tonight, water persistent and immense
> that raises the streams and begins to swell the rivers,
> which groan with their nocturnal burden of vegetal sludge.
>
> The rain on the zinc rooftops
> chants its presence and drives away sleep,
> to leave me in a flood of restless waters,
> in the fresh, fresh night that spills
> through the vault of the coffee trees
> and slides down the sickly trunk of the giant balsas.
>
> Now, suddenly, in the middle of the night
> the rain has returned to the coffee groves
> and amidst the vegetal cry of the waters

Opposite: Mangrove forest, Ensenada de Utría National Park Chocó.

Gonzalo Ariza. *Coffee grove*, oil painting, 110 x 155 cm.

Along every route in the center of the country one can track down such great events, but on the margins the vast landscape gives testimony to something that the poet Auden once pointed out, namely, that the main difference between the Old World and the New is that in Europe, however lost a person may find himself, he is always near some centuries-old city, whereas every American has seen with his own eyes regions that are practically untouched by history.

the stuff of other days reaches me untouched,
saved from the alien work of the passing years.

At Coello you begin the climb to Cajamarca. From tropical forests of *carboneros* that crowd the slopes, passing through the town trapped between defiles, and in the presence of a distant, white waterfall in the center of an unreal landscape, you reach the great abysses of La Línea and, high above, whether there is sun or mist, see hundreds of wax palms, with their straight white stems which burst, at the top, into a delicate black star of leaves. On the high passes, on clear days, you can spy the basin of the Quindío River, which forms part of the departments of the Quindío, Risaralda and Caldas. They were still virgin lands a century and a half ago, untouched since the time the Indians were annihilated, and, less than half a century ago, still belonged to the region known as viejo (old) Caldas: a mountainous area of sugar cane plots and rustic sugar mills, the region, now celebrated as the "axis of Colombian coffee", where the colonization by settlers from Antioquia was most intense.

We dizzyingly descend from the foggy summits of La Línea, on the volcanic Central Cordillera, to Calarcá and Armenia. Where, before, there were forests, we now find symmetrical plantations of coffee, barely shaded by *guamo* trees and plantains, the country's main source of wealth for decades: temperate, fertile lands, rich in flowers, and beyond them, the plains of Caicedonia, with their distant views of edenic palm groves, fern-filled paths and woods, where you see ash-colored *yarumo* trees whose outspread leaves seem like streaks of silver against the dark trees.

There thus arrives the descent to the Valle del Cauca, once again under the violent tropical light: broad prairies interrupted in the distance by the remote, blue wall of the rocky outcrops to the west, the cordillera of vertical basalt walls behind which rage the storms of the Pacific. This is the valley of Jorge Isaac's *María*, which is not only a story of romantic love, but also a meticulous description of what this region of America was like in the mid-19th century: its landscapes, life on its great haciendas, its peasant-farmers, the dangers of hunting its jaguars, the human struggle against an unbridled nature, the riders who crossed swollen rivers at midnight, who rode down through the canyons of the River Dagua, amidst enormous cliffs, mosses and ferns and the purest of waters, as they endeavored to penetrate the valley from the hard- to -reach wharf of Buenaventura, the main port of the Pacific.

The plain is not as full of *ceibas* and *samanes*, of flowers and fruit trees, as it formerly was, but you perceive the aroma of ripe mangoes in the wind. Rows of flowering *mataratones* succeed one another, and there are also *caracolíes* and the low *chiminangos* that sometimes give the landscape an air of Africa, with stretches of soy bean, sorghum and cotton plantations and, above all, sugar cane. It is the region of great sugar mills. Here, everything looks like the interior of Cuba – the fields, the crowds of black and mulatto cane cutters, the smell of sugar cane block (*panela*) in the wind. And at this end of this

---

Desert of La Guajira.

Confinement in Andean villages and in ports closed off from the world sent the country into a long sleep, under the illusion that it was alone, daily emerging from the earth, like a plant, and later returning to it, without the slightest contact with the outside world.

150 Valley of Cocora. Quindío.

Opposite: Rapids of the Tuparro River. Tuparro National Natural Park. Vichada.

This oppressive dynamic of a nature which is too active, too vigorous, which is insolently fecund, was a hellish experience for the Spanish conquistadors when they penetrated the wilds of the equinoctial regions in the ingenuous belief that America would be the same as the gentle lands of Europe.

journey through all the emotions that landscape may provide, there is Cali, stretching beyond the River Cauca to approach the first ridges on the west.

Cali, with its long, palm-shaded neighborhoods; its districts where the joyful offspring of Africa live; its old streets perfumed at dusk by the aroma of *camias* and *guayacanes* which shower their purple flowers on the avenues; its street-corner vendors of red *chontaduro*-palm nuts; its salsa discotheques that come alive at night; its heavy dog days and burning river banks and the sensuality you feel as evening falls, when the fresh breeze which blows through the canyons from the ocean turns Cali into the only coastal city that is not on the sea: a Caribbean city, you might say, set into the valleys of the interior, next to the dense and humid jungle of the Pacific.

Aware that space is continually modified by time, in *One hundred years of solitude* Gabriel García Márquez often delights in showing us the same landscape at different historical periods. When the men of Macondo go in search of civilization, we observe the discovery of an old Spanish vessel run aground far from the sea:

> In front of them, surrounded by ferns and palms, white and dusty in the silent morning light, was an enormous Spanish galleon, slightly leaning to starboard. From its intact rigging hung pale scraps of the sails, amid the rigging adorned with orchids. The hull, covered by a smooth armor-plating of petrified remora and tender moss, was firmly embedded in the stony soil. The whole structure seemed to occupy an ambit of its own, a space of solitude and oblivion, spared the blemishes of time and the habits of birds. In the interior, which the members of the expedition explored with a stealthy fervor, there was nothing more than a dense forest of flowers.

No sooner have we delighted in this splendid description, verbal and visual at the same time, than the writer takes the liberty of showing us the same place at a later time:

> Many years later, colonel Aureliano Buendía crossed the region again, when it was already a regular mail route, and all that he found of the vessel was its charred ribs in the middle of a field of poppies.

We would need an author like García Márquez to portray what this route we have just traveled over – between the savanna and the Valle de Cauca – was like in different historical periods. To tell us what it was like in the irretrievable times of indigenous America: starting from the country of the Chibchas, with their cornfields, burnished frogs of gold and blocks of salt; descending to the land of the potters of Tolima and the fierce Pijaos; climbing again over the dizzying slopes to the country of the Quimbayas, with their golden breastplates; and finally descending to the region of the Calimas and the plains where the master gold-workers of Malagana culture brought a great refinement to their figures of crickets and birds.

Opposite: El Valle, Chocó.

Pages 154-155: Mompox, Bolívar.

The journey from Cali to Buenaventura doesn't take more than three hours either, but what a wealth of landscapes stretch out! From the exceptionally fertile valley of the Cauca, crossing the canyons of the Dagua and the cliffs of the Western Cordillera, to reach those flooded lands of the coastal jungles: from the region of palms to the tangled mangrove swamps on the seashore.

Or to tell us how it was at the beginning of the 19th century, when Humboldt set out from the savanna and the savant José Celestino Mutis directed the work, scientific and artistic at the same time, of the Royal Botanical Expedition, studies complemented by splendid color plates. To tell us what the banks of the River Magdalena would have been like, at that small port that was still not called Girardot, where butterflies perched on the slimy backs of caimans. To tell us what this exuberant American world said to Humboldt when he saw the wax palms and mist forests and the basin of the Quindío, glimpsed the ash-colored *yarumos* in the cordillera and vainly sought the undiscovered flower of the *guadua* bamboo, which he only came across, months later, in the hills of Popayán.

To tell us what it said to him while he rested in the viceroy's house in Cartago, which had been built for him without anyone knowing it, and crossed the flooded stretches of the Valle del Cauca. Or to tell us what the same landscape was like in 1812, when Nariño set off from the savanna at the head of an army of men from Cundinamarca, Boyacá and Antioquia: an army that imperceptibly shrank as it advanced through the canyons of Fusa, crossed the River Magdalena, made camp in the prairies of Melgar; those troops with which Nariño dreamt of stopping the advance from the south of the Spanish reconquest. That army which was blotted out by the mists of the Central Cordillera to reappear, even more meager, amid the dense ferns of the Quindío, and when it reached the Valley of the Cauca, where it waged several desperate battles, seemed to definitively lose its ardor. To the south, there awaited the mass desertion of the troops, afraid to tackle the canyon of the Patía, where Indian warriors stalked them at every bend of the river, to the point where, having crossed the canyon, the general arrived with only two thousand men and had to surrender to the royalist troops.

Along every route in the center of the country one can track down such great events, but on the margins the vast landscape gives testimony to something that the poet Auden once pointed out, namely, that the main difference between the Old World and the New is that in Europe, however lost a person may find himself, he is always near some centuries-old city, whereas every American has seen with his own eyes regions that are practically untouched by history. You have only to think of the dense jungles of the Darien Gap, which close off the trail to the isthmus of Panama. Of the vast stretch of marshes in the north or the dense tropical forests of Turbaco. Of the canyon of the Chicamocha and the paramos of Pamplona. Of the rocky outcrops of Cali, whose blue walls separate the central body of the country from the jungles of the west and the stretch of the Southern Sea, that endless ocean that stands between the original Americans and their Asian birthplace. Of the inclined plains of Herveo, next to the Ruiz volcano; of the windy gorges of the Sierra Nevada; of the canyon of the Patía; of the paramos of Choachí and the eastern cliffs of the savanna. Of the Sierra del Cocuy, in the Macarena range, and the vast stretches of the Casanare, or the immense jungles of the Guaviare, Vaupés and Amazon, eaten away today by our industrial society, but protected for millennia by the myths of the tree of all fruits and the starry skin of the great anaconda.

Opposite: Narrows of the Magdalena River. Huila.

Pages 158-159: Field of sorghum. Yotoco, Valle del Cauca.

Perhaps there is no causal link, but it is curious that the word Colombia, monument to a strong individuality, should be the name of a country that tends to worship the individual. Nobody can tell us what kind of psychological or mythical effect names may have on their communities: descriptive names like Argentina or Costa Rica, religious ones like El Salvador or names that lack any poetic color, like the United States.

COLOMBIA

Two hundred years ago the word "Colombia" was only an idea in the mind of a young man from Caracas who was witnessing the birth of the republics of Europe and dreamt of also shaping republics out of the barely conquered clay of America. The youngster had inherited this dream from a daring Venezuelan, Francisco de Miranda, who had traveled through Europe, pondering and fighting, an important French Revolutionary general whose name is engraved on the Arc de Triomphe in Paris and was, legend has it, the lover of the Tsarina of Russia. The young Bolívar came to understand that nations are not always the fruit of a very long traditions but may be historical constructions, the result of an encounter between a philosophy, and a territory and a number of communities.

That is what happened with the union in North America, where a vast territory prepared itself for great historical enterprises guided by the principle of democracy, the ideal government by majority that was based on the premise of an essential equality among human beings. It happened thus with Spain, which after ten thousand *mestizajes* had chosen to define itself as the Iberian nation grouped around the Castilian language, Catholic religion and unified crown of Aragon and Castile. To reach that idea of nationality, arbitrary but doubtless possible, the Catholic Monarchs drove the Moors from the peninsula, the Moors whose civilization had inhabited the south for seven centuries and had left its clarity in their architecture, its hospitality in their customs and its sweetness in the many words that were incorporated forever into the Spanish language; and expelled the Jews, who had contributed to the country their long memory, tenacity and fatalism. To be able to construct modern republics in the lands of America, there was no doubt that it was necessary to defeat and expel the peninsular Spanish, who kept even their own offspring born in America in a subordinate state and gave everything they organized in this land the sole function of benefiting the mother country.

The young man from Caracas was a typical child of his times. From the perspective of the dawn of the 21st century, we might say that he was a Romantic and the truth is that few men of that age better embodied the spirit of that vital movement that was called Romanticism.

He had been reared in the pedagogical precepts of Jean Jacques Rousseau, the solitary, pensive stroller who infected the 19th century with a novel cult of nature and a yearning for political transformations that came to be the source of great

Opposite: Pedro José Figueroa. *Bolívar with allegorical figure of Indian woman representing America*, 1819, oil on canvas. 125 x 95 cm. Quinta de Bolívar. Bogotá.

Pages 162-163: José María Espinosa. *Battle of río Palo* (detail), 1850, oil on canvas. 81 x 121 cm. Museo Nacional de Colombia.

In this world which is so ancient a nation which received its current name barely two centuries ago and only started using it a century and a half ago catches one's attention.

radical movements. Rousseau was a prophet for the boys of that energetic generation, but each interpreted him in his own way. From the fearful Robespierre, who exalted him on the banner of violent Jacobinism, a symbol of the creed of virtue and terror, to the gentle Friedrich Hölderlin, who found in him a mystical lover of nature and the great prophet of the upheavals that would shake the world in that unruly *fin de siecle*.

Bolívar was also a reader of the Enlightenment philosophers, European by culture but spiritually enriched by his American origin and Creole status, a lucid writer and generous warrior who came to be a legend throughout the Western hemisphere. In Italy, during the second decade of the 19th century, one of the greatest Romantic heroes of the Europe of that time, the English poet George Gordon Byron, not only insistently proclaimed his wish to enroll in the ranks of Bolívar to fight for the independence of Colombia, but also named the boat in which he sailed around the bay of Spezia, on the Italian coast, "Bolívar".

It is curious, this capacity of certain human beings to impregnate a world with their spirit and leave their mark on everything they touch. When you visit Santa Marta, the joyful city that stretches between the mysterious Sierra Nevada mountains and the Caribbean sea, you will find, in the middle of a splendid wood, the old mansion of San Pedro Alejandrino, with its four-hundred year-old *ceiba* and *bonga* trees to which the dying Bolívar tied his hammock so that he could sleep as he had on his military campaigns, and the solemn and austere bedroom where he listened to the voices and winds of the world for the last time. This hacienda, which reminds us how these lands were several centuries ago, with enormous trees that modernity has wiped out everywhere and extensive native forests, continues to commemorate the name of Bolívar, although "el Libertador" only spent the last eleven days of his life there. Eleven days that were sufficient to erase everything else that might have happened in that place in the course of the centuries.

The Colombia that Bolívar dreamt of was vaster than the nation which bears that name today. It included the isthmus of Panama, where the Liberator was eager to found the capital of a continental union of republics (the same place that Humboldt and Goethe later recommended as the best route for an inter-oceanic canal). It included Venezuela, his own country, where he had been born into the Creole cocoa-bean aristocracy, whose members were as powerful and well-known in Europe as the merchants of Veracruz, the silver miners of northern Mexico, the powerful sugar-mill owners of Havana, the magnates of Potosí and the slave traders of Buenos Aires.

It included Ecuador, the northernmost part of the ancient Inca empire, and a considerable part of the Amazon basin. And, of course, it included the central zone bordering on all of those geographical marvels, which was the Vice-Royalty of Nueva Granada, the northwest corner of South America, which boasted of the

Opposite: *Atlas* dedicated to Jorge Tadeo Lozano, drawn by Francisco José de Caldas, 1811.

Pages 166-167: Quinta de San Pedro Alejandrino (the country house where Bolívar died). Santa Marta, Magdalena.

When you visit Santa Marta, the joyful city that stretches between the mysterious Sierra Nevada mountains and the Caribbean sea, you will find, in the middle of a splendid wood, the old mansion of San Pedro Alejandrino, with its four-hundred year-old ceiba and bonga trees to which the dying Bolívar tied his hammock so that he could sleep as he had on his military campaigns, and the solemn and austere bedroom where he listened to the voices and winds of the world for the last time.

legendary fortress of Cartagena de Indias on its Caribbean coast, the region crossed by the triple cordillera into which the Andes divide before disappearing into the prairies of the Caribbean.

The romantic Bolívar, who loved poetry as much the sword, combined the virtues of the dreamer and the practical man, and his writings, done in an admirable literary style, are still a good testimony to the spirit of foresight that he always had. He knew that, thus unified, this territory might become one of the richest and most influential countries of the continent, and that its extraordinary agricultural and mineral wealth, its natural resources, jungles, rivers and oceans, together with its human resources and strategic position, might enable a great nation to come into being. Once independence from Spanish power was attained – the nation that had kept these lands in the condition of tax-paying subordinates and had benefited from their wealth without ever seriously trying to grant them a worthy place in the concert of nations – surely the American themselves would be capable of quickly learning the arts of government and the secrets of administration and organize their very rich world in an efficient and modern way.

He did not forget to warn that there would be difficulties for such a unification. Although the different territories shared a recent history marked by the same tragedies and heroic feats, the way in which their peoples had gradually fused into different nations already gave each of them singular features, and when there is neither a strong philosophy nor a higher philosophy to guide them, nations have to fall back on their particular character. Bolívar had tried to provide this philosophy, but the cause was too vast, the problems to be resolved too numerous and the interests to be reconciled too complex for the work of a single man or a few men to be able to blaze the trail for a whole world.

The people of North America had had to deal with a huge and complex territory but their colonial period did not leave them such a conflictive and deeply-rooted legacy of privilege and discrimination as that which the South Americans faced at the time when they proclaimed their independence. To this very day the eloquent critics of a state of things that has changed little since those times, allow themselves, with the healthy lack of inhibition and irreverence that are typical of our societies, to reproach those liberating patriots and founding fathers for having made a bad job of their mission. In his novel *El fuego secreto* (The secret fire), the impassioned and often unfair Fernando Vallejo cries out against Bolívar in the following words: "The Liberator, they tell us, but what did he free us from? From Spain and its pen-pushers? From those who change the mayor, the procurator, the treasurer, the governor, the minister every two months? They do it to be fair, to be just, because you have to share out the loot, the meager bone that we took from the Spaniard more than one hundred and fifty years ago, now bodiless for so much snarling".

He is partly right: despite the Independence, the great landlords, heirs of a seigniorial system that in the eastern region of the country was run by *encomenderos*, the

Monument to the Heroes of the Independence. Bogotá.

Pages 170-171: San Fernando de Bocachica Fort. Cartagena, Bolívar.

Bolívar was also a reader of the Enlightenment philosophers, European by culture but spiritually enriched by his American origin and Creole status, a lucid writer and generous warrior who came to be a legend throughout the Western hemisphere.

beneficiaries of Crown grants that gave them feudal rights over the labor of countless Indians (but, in theory, without titles to the land), and in the western region, by the masters of legions of Black slaves. These magnates conserved their power and their lands, while others seized hold of them during the anarchy of the Independence, while the clergy held onto most of the privileges which it had acquired during three centuries of colonial domination. The social stratifications had been defined and fossilized century after century and the rushed Independence never undertook the job of correcting these centuries-old evils, because it only sought to modify the social contract in terms of the question of who would inherit the power of the *peninsulares* (the Spanish). It was not concerned with the construction of a different social order, one that would be in line with the democratic philosophy which Bolívar and Nariño had inherited from their Enlightenment teachers, their rationalist philosophers and their Romantic poets – something that was unlikely to spread to the rich local notabilities who were going to benefit from that historic change.

To begin with, it was those same powers and those same Creole worthies who thwarted the dream of the country which Bolívar had in mind. A second rank of generals fought, instead, to build comfortable pocket republics. Páez did it to his Venezuela, Flórez to his Ecuador and Santander to his Colombia, and each found arguments to legitimize this hurried secession which diluted the country of Gran Colombia (Great Colombia) when Bolívar had barely been laid in his grave. While Bolívar was gradually being undermined by illness, adversity and disillusion, his continental dream was likewise being undermined by local and factional interests, by the ambitions of soldiers and politicians much less farseeing than he, who lost sight of the world and the epoch, and yielded to the intoxication of being the administrators or oppressors of a number of village-states.

We must remind ourselves, over and over again, that our countries are inconceivable without modernity and contact with the rest of the world. In current times, there are very few communities which may claim the privilege of belonging to a tradition that is self-enclosed, the master of its own, exclusive cosmogony, language, philosophy, system of myths, dress, ornamental style, medicine, ancestral space and magical universe. It is true, of course, that present-day Colombia has some of these communities among its components, full of cultural treasures, deeply rooted in a territory over centuries, possessors of a wisdom that will be surely be vital for our future, for it holds some of the clues to the survival of our planet. But without losing sight of the value of those communities, of the indigenous societies which inhabit our land and are a source of pride for us, Colombia is a Mestizo nation, equally inconceivable without the culture of classical Greece, without the Roman Empire, without the Latin Middle Ages, without the Arab emirates of Córdoba, without the Spanish empire, without the Vatican, without the European Renaissance, without the Spanish "siglo de oro" (Golden Age), without the adventures

Opposite: Front curtain, work by Aníbal Gutti. Cristóbal Colón Theater. Bogotá.

Pages 174-175: Inner courtyard of the National Capitol and statue of Rafael Núñez. Bogotá.

There are countless traditions in the world to which we do not belong and many nations with which we have no direct historical link, but the influences which I have just enumerated had a decisive weight in the formation of our country, our mentality and our dreams: they form an undeniable part of the past and present of which we are made.

of the Dutch, English and Spanish on the coasts of Africa, without the offspring of Guinea, Mali, Angola and the Ivory Coast, without the British pirates, without the Enlightenment, without the French Revolution, without German Rationalism, without the Napoleonic wars, without English Liberalism, without the automobile factories of the United States, without the Symbolism of the French poets, without the imperatives of "comfort" which rule today and also threaten the contemporary consumer society.

There are countless traditions in the world to which we do not belong and many nations with which we have no direct historical link, but the influences which I have just enumerated had a decisive weight in the formation of our country, our mentality and our dreams: they form an undeniable part of the past and present of which we are made. The traits, language, literature, morality, laws, institutions, customs, hopes and faults that characterize us are fed by that long and complex river of intermingled cultural traditions. Every time that we ask ourselves who we are and what Colombia is, we must examine those complex origins, evident in a number of highly visible elements and symbols: the Spanish language enriched by the American experience; the religion of Christ highly tinged by our triple indigenous, European and African universe; republican institutions greatly modified by the system of party bosses and the seigniorial spirit bequeathed to us by the Colony, which perpetuated and sophisticated their defects under a republican disguise; mestizo individualism, based on a suspicion of all law, a generalized willingness to transgress it and a dangerous predominance of the private over the public; a lax and mocking morality that is lucidly wary of systems but wastes itself on Pyrrhic or disastrous rebellions; a vigorous culture of fusions that is more rich, more surprising and more promising every day.

The name of Colombia stayed with us, and with it, the hard certainty of complex origins which we have never been fully able to face up to. No name is trivial and much less the one which a nation adopts as its own. For some, the weight of tradition defines everything and to call yourself Mexico or England is to seek the foundation of a historical identity in the paternal or mythical tutelage of the Mexicas or Angles. Naturally, all the names of nations have had a beginning and were incorporated into their tradition and history at a specific time. For a long time, France had to be called Galias (Latin for Gaul) and was later the poetical country of Oil and then Oc, before the angels of the forest placed it in the martial hands of Joan of Arc.

Iraq is a testimony to the passage of time, since over the centuries its territory witnessed a succession of some of the legendary kingdoms of the world: the Ottoman empire was there and before that the Roman empire and before that the empire of Alexander and before that Persia and Assyria and Mesopotamia and Chaldea, which discovered the stars in the sky. Niger is the Latin word for black and Liberia owes its name to the freed slaves from the United States who filially returned to the Africa of their forefathers, with the help of President Monroe, to whom the capital,

Ignacio Gómez Jaramillo. *Freeing of the slaves* (detail), 1938, fresco. 326 x 306 cm. National Capitol. Bogotá.

The name of Colombia stayed with us, and with it, the hard certainty of complex origins which we have never been fully able to face up to. No name is trivial and much less the one which a nation adopts as its own.

Monrovia, owes its name. In this world which is so ancient a nation which received its current name barely two centuries ago and only started using it a century and a half ago catches one's attention. Venezuela was called by that name since the Conquest, Ecuador owes its name to a geographical convention that rightly corresponds to it and each of the United States of America has its historic name, although in that immense country where no one is, strictly speaking, a native, no one forgets the tradition he belongs to or where his past lies.

But it is significant when the name of a country does not come from a part of its territory nor the appellative of a tribe or people, but from a historical personage. Perhaps there is no better example of the triumph of the idea of the individual in contemporary society than this fact of granting a country the name of a person. It is a forceful consequence of that typically modern event, the discovery of America, and in line with the circumstance that the whole continent was given the name of a voyager who lived five centuries ago, an arbitrary homage paid to a figure of secondary importance rather than its true discoverer. This ostensible ingratitude was what Bolívar wished to correct by giving our land the name of the Admiral and thus perpetuate his memory.

One wonders whether Bolívar might not have asked himself if it made real sense to give a country a name not hallowed by a long tradition and not even connected with its land, but the result of a historical accident. One philosopher urged scientists to utilize Greek and Latin roots to name their discoveries and thus link the new with tradition. This did not prevent one of the discoverers of the six subatomic particles from deciding to use the word "quark" to name one of them, a literary onomatopoeia drawn from the pages of James Joyce's *Finnegan's Wake*. Giving the extremely ancient substance of the world – America being a geographical reality, above all – a name as recent and individual as Colombia is a strange practice, but it is a centuries-old fact by now. Many generations have adopted it as their own name, turned it into part of their identity, sung its praises and tried to elevate it to the realm of mythology, as every nation needs to.

In our land poets and novelists frequently refuse to use the relevant geographical and historical names, which still seem superficial and nearly provisional to us, and invent names that better fulfill the mythical function that one expects of them. This, said the poet Auden, has been more of an American than a European habit, and the names which American writers have given to their cities or worlds seem to respond to that longing to create fabled, magical regions that are not polluted by the provisional and the immediate nature of our world: Lovecraft's Auber's Tarn, Faulkner's Yoknapatawpha County, Gárcia Márquez's village of Macondo, Borges' country of Uqbar and planet Tlön, and Barba Jacob's city of Acuarimántima

Recently, however, our writers have increasingly learned to name their land. Perhaps the irruption of new artistic values makes it possible to enter into this dealing with

G. P. Dagrant de Burdeos. *Allegory of the Republic*, stained glass, Salón Boyacá, National Capitol. Bogotá.

The romantic Bolívar, who loved poetry as much the sword, combined the virtues of the dreamer and the practical man, and his writings, done in an admirable literary style, are still a good testimony to the spirit of foresight that he always had. He knew that, thus unified, this territory might become one of the richest and most influential countries of the continent, and that its extraordinary agricultural and mineral wealth, its natural resources, jungles, rivers and oceans, together with its human resources and strategic position, might enable a great nation to come into being.

reality, values which do not seek strangeness but recognition. Thus, Faulkner also delighted in the name of Alabama and Tennessee. García Márquez does not miss an opportunity to evoke his mythical Cartagena de Indias, the perpetual winds of the Guajira, the city of Riohacha and the Ciénaga Grande marshlands.

Borges also writes about Buenos Aires, about the towns of Adrogué and Fray Bentos. Barba Jacob does not ignore the poetry of Sayula, Sopetrán and Santa Rosa de Osos. It was he who also said, nearly for the first time in a truly poetic tone – that is, free of patriotic effusions:

> The numen of Colombia gave me a lovely rose,
> but I asked for the twilight and was greedy for the star.

It is curious that the word Colombia, monument to a strong individuality, should be the name of a country that tends to worship the individual. Nobody can tell us what kind of psychological or mythical effect names may have on their communities: descriptive names like Argentina or Costa Rica, religious ones like El Salvador or names that lack any poetic color, like the United States.

Opposite: San Bernardo del Viento, Córdoba.

Below: Prairies of the Casanare.

Pages 182-183: Plaza de Armas, Casa de Nariño (Presidential Palace). Bogotá.

In our land poets and novelists frequently refuse to use geographical and historical names, which still seem superficial and nearly provisional to them, but invent names that better suit the mythical role expected of them.

CITIES AND REGIONS

That rural country run by priests and landlords which entered the 20th century with four million inhabitants broke apart with the partisan violence of the 1950's and the dramatic flight of millions of peasant-farmers to the cities. The cyclic symbol of exile marked our emergence as a modern community, our entrance into the republican system and the world market, and our subjection to the political arrangements of the century, but that fratricidal war, generally known as "the Violence" (*la Violencia*), produced a drastic rupture of our historical memory and gave an ill-fated course to the future.

A song from the 1950's became a kind of national litany for Colombians. Called *Las acacias* (The Acacia trees), it was a melancholy description of the old house of a family of a peasant-farmers which had been abandoned. Everyone had left it: "some dead, and others alive whose soul had died". That expression of the tragedy in common language had a profound resonance in the quite different languages of art and literature: in *La casa grande* (The big house), by Álvaro Cepeda Samudio; *Cien años de soledad*; *Morada al sur*, the great poem by Aurelio Arturo; *Vana Stanza* (Vain Stanza), by Amílcar Osorio; *Exilio* (Exile), by Álvaro Mutis, and in a way that was hilarious and despairing at the same time, Fernando Vallejo's novel, *El desbarrancadero* (The precipice). It was also seen in films like *La estrategia del caracol* (The strategy of the snail), by Sergio Cabrera or Victor Gaviria's *La vendedora de rosas* (The rose seller).

In five decades Colombia turned not only into an urban country but one of cities. Many visitors are surprised by the variety of these cities and their surrounding regions. By the walled coastal city of Cartagena de Indias, with the narrow streets, beautiful mansions and quaint balconies of its colonial center and the big, modern beach resort district of Bocagrande, which form a contrast with the enormous, agonizing and somehow invisible slums on the periphery which spread into the surrounding countryside.

By the city of the plain, Cali, silhouetted against the blue wall of the cliffs to the west, with its perfumed vegetation, songs that celebrate the beauty of its women, tropical languor by day and frenzied rumba by night; with its history of seigniorial haciendas and the joyful street cries of its mulatto inhabitants, with its violence and sensuality. And also the vast slums full of those displaced from the countryside by poverty or violence.

Then there is the famous industrial center, Medellín, the tireless and hard-working city of the mountains, with the slums which dizzily climb its eastern and western flanks

Center of Bogotá, from the eastern ridges.

Page 186: Clock Tower. Cartagena, Bolívar.

Page 187: Monument to Sebastián de Belalcázar. Cali, Valle del Cauca.

In five decades Colombia turned not only into an urban country but one of cities. Many visitors are surprised by the variety of these cities and their surrounding regions.

By the walled coastal city of Cartagena de Indias, with the narrow streets, beautiful mansions and quaint balconies of its colonial center and the big, modern beach resort district of Bocagrande, which form a contrast with the enormous, agonizing and somehow invisible slums on the periphery which spread into the surrounding countryside. By the city of the plain, Cali, silhouetted against the blue wall of the cliffs to the west, with its perfumed vegetation, songs that celebrate the beauty of its women, tropical languor by day and frenzied rumba by night; with its history of seigniorial haciendas and the joyful street cries of its mulatto inhabitants, with its violence and sensuality.

Opposite:
La Alpujarra administrative center and sculpture by Rodrigo Arenas Betancourt. Medellín.

Pages 190-191: Kite Festival. Villa de Leiva, Boyacá.

and neighborhoods of tall modern buildings on densely-wooded hills. It is the capital of the region which has most figured in Colombian literature, from the delightful, observant, colloquial style of the short-story writer Tomás Carrasquilla to the fierce imprecations of the novelist Fernando Vallejo; from the clamorous, poignant poetry of Barba Jacob to the austere revelations of José Manuel Arango.

Barranquilla stretches between the sea and the River Magdalena, a city of spacious neighborhoods united by its passion for its famous Carnivals. Nearby is the long wharf of Puerto Colombia, which was the gateway to Colombia for travelers in the golden years of the early 20th century and for a few immigrants, the Syrian-Lebanese and Germans who fleetingly opened the country to the winds of modernity.

Popayán is the city where you most clearly see the three races of which we are composed. It is a Spanish-style urban center where you nevertheless increasingly note the presence of the colorfully-dressed Guambiano and Paéz Indians. A city with a fierce statue of the conquistador who founded it on its highest hill, proud of its peaceful ridges, magnificent churches, immense houses with stone-paved courtyards and colonnades, and the enormous home of its heraldic poet Guillermo Valencia – a city torn between being the center of a seignorial world and its more ancient condition as the center of an indigenous, black and mulatto world, and recently discovering its closeness to the sea. The city from which there arose the marmoreal poetry of Valencia, but also the inward and impassioned verses of Rafael Maya:

> At last thou hast forgotten me, what gentle and heartfelt oblivion,
> After the undefined boundary of our dark past,
> The star that watched over the two of us has fallen,
> Like a dark tear that shatters when it falls…

And where the melodious and magical poetry of Giovanni Quessup, that offspring of the Caribbean and Lebanon, sought refuge in the hills and silence.

> Who has set out in earnest
> to sing in the night and at these hours?
> Who has lost sleep and seeks it in music and shadow?
> What says this song interwoven
> of cypress branches in the coppice?
> Woe betide the man who fashions his soul from these leaves,
> And of these leaves fashions his chimeras!
> Where dost thou come from, madrigal,
> which hast turned everything into bewitched grief?
> Poor me!, who listens to thee in the penumbra.
> The song that keeps me awake is gone.

Then there is the famous industrial center, Medellín, the tireless and hard-working city of the mountains, with the slums which dizzily climb its eastern and western flanks and neighborhoods of tall modern buildings on densely-wooded hills. It is the capital of the region which has most figured in Colombian literature, from the delightful, observant, colloquial style of the short-story writer Tomás Carrasquilla to the fierce imprecations of the novelist Fernando Vallejo; from the clamorous, poignant poetry of Barba Jacob to the austere revelations of José Manuel Arango.

Next is the city of vertigo built on the cornices of the Andes, Manizales, which, instead of concealing nature, bares all of its contours, following the capricious outlines of the mountains, as though to challenge the classical notion of the city, a city where you can see the slums on different levels, one following another on the slopes as they scale the heights.

And on the central savanna, Bogotá, which never stops growing and invading the fertile plain around it, which seems to endlessly flee from itself, a city originally built alongside its eastern mountain ridges – green and wooded north of Monserrate, dark and stony south of Guadalupe – but now stretched in squares over the level ground and spilling over the arid mountains of the south. That capital whose phosphorescent stain advances in all directions by night and devours the neighboring towns. Bogotá, with its slender towers and labyrinthine districts on the heights, tutelary high Andean moors and indigenous mythologies, Gold Museum and the precious collection of contemporary art donated by Fernando Botero. Bogotá, with its traditional English-style neighborhoods and crowded redbrick buildings, history of republican betrayals and grammarian rulers, remembrances of impulsive poets, noisy orators and disdainful aristocrats, dozens of universities and big libraries. Bogotá, with the indifference, opulence, poverty and crime that flow through its crowded avenues at 2,600 meters above sea level.

And then there are Bucaramanga and Pereira and Armenia and Pasto and Neiva, a long list of cities in which 80% of the population of Colombia lives today, which suffer the tragedy of an incomplete urbanization, of a brusque rupture with the countryside, of a mental outlook that is taking a long time to become contemporary and a long time to become truly democratic.

At the end of the 19th century Colombia was still divided into six, clearly distinguishable regions, which partly corresponded to what had been the member states from 1863 till 1886 of a federation called the Estados Unidos de Colombia.

The whole of the northern coast, which Colombians call the Costa Atlántica today, made up the states of Bolívar and el Magdalena. It stretched from the deserts of the Guajira – a yellow expanse next to the blue of the Caribbean where you find the white deposits of salt of Manaure and the black deposits of coal of El Cerrejón –, ran through the nearby Sierra Nevada de Santa Marta – the world's highest coastal mountain, with forty rivers running down its slopes –, the lowlands where the river Magdalena debouches, close to Barranquilla, and the vast region of marshes that forms the mythological world of García Márquez, and reached Cartagena, the walled city that withstood the sieges of English pirates from the 16th century onwards.

Cartagena, the city of Germán Espinosa's novel, *La tejedora de coronas* (The woman who weaves crowns), the fortress that witnessed the arrival of enormous cargoes of slaves and the shipwreck of the great galleons off its islands. From there the state of the Magdalena ran south through the region of marshes and the home of the still

Calle 80, Bogotá.

The cyclic symbol of exile marked our emergence as a modern community, our entrance into the republican system and the world market, and our subjection to the political arrangements of the century, but that fratricidal war, generally known as "the Violence" (la Violencia), produced a drastic rupture of our historical memory and gave an ill-fated course to the future.

194 Above: Guadua bamboo groves and mountains. Caldas.

Below: Gorgona Island, Pacific Ocean.

Above: Chiles, Nariño.

Below: Puerto Carreño, Vichada.

popular folkloric songs known as *vallenatos*; west through the region of the Sinú, a place of indigenous temples in the past and cattle haciendas now. The third state was the isthmus of Panama, which Colombia lost in 1903

To the east lay the state of Santander, a harsh region of rugged mountains and beautiful cities and villages. In the north, amidst the storax-groves, there is the city of Cúcuta, hidden in its trees. From there you ascend to the paramos of Pamplona, the city which Pedro de Ursúa founded during a pause in the fierce wars he fought four centuries ago, and pass through the tablelands to reach Bucaramanga, another great provincial capital, known for the beautiful vegetation of its parks. South of it are a succession of celebrated and peaceful towns: San Gil – which also has magnificent trees –, Barichara, with its rich stone architecture, Socorro and Barbosa, following the course of that branch of the Andes which stretches to Venezuela and spreads over two departments today.

Santander is the land of the valiant colonial rebellion of "los Comuneros", one of the vigorous forerunners of the Independence. Formerly known for its large plantations of tobacco and *quina* (cinchona) bark, it is a region of hardworking craftsmen and prosperous industries, where farms alternate with oil fields and the visitor is astounded by one of the most formidable wilderness areas of the American world, the canyon of the Chicamocha, a region worthy of the Last Judgment, where your gaze becomes lost as it follows the dry and violent flanks of the mountains. From there you descend to the burning plains of the Magdalena, where the refinery city of Barrancabermeja stands, a place of blazing oil wells surrounded by large cattle ranches. In former times, as you followed the winding course of the small rivers of this area, you were sure to find great stretches of virgin forest, with legions of mischievous monkeys in the trees and flocks of parrots making a row at dusk.

The fifth state was Antioquia, perhaps the most dynamic of all, a region of small farms and hardworking families of whites and mestizos with deep-rooted religious sentiments, of astute and enterprising men. It was here that Medellín was founded and grew, the country's second city and most homogeneous and go-getting one, with a mythology that revolves around being industrious and sharp; a place of pioneering businessmen and violent slums where some of the country's most important industrial concerns rose to prominence in the course of the 20th century and there also flourished, towards the end of it, a powerful drugs cartel known for its cruelty and crimes.

It was from these prolific smallholdings that there emerged the waves of pioneers who carried out the "Antioquian colonization" of virgin lands from the middle of the 19th century onwards. They settled the mountains in the center of the country, in what is now the coffee zone of north Tolima, the northern part of el Valle, Risaralda, Quindío and Caldas, the latter the center of the colonization, where the city of Manizales stands.

Opposite: Jungle of el Chocó.

Pages 198-199: Tota lake, Boyacá.

In the jungles the close-packed trees do not let in the light of day; in the mountains the mist produces, in broad daylight, that disturbing phenomenon, the white-out, places where everything is invisible; in the hot climates the fierce rainstorms blot out the world.

200

Right, above:
Cabo de la Vela.
La Guajira.

Right, below:
Valley of Cocora.
Salento, Quindío.

Opposite, above:
Desert of la Tatacoa.
Huila.

Opposite, below:
Morgan's Head,
Island of
Providencia.

The anomalous reality of Colombia, its capricious history, led to the growth of ruling classes who gave the impression of being European, with very precise notions about Paris and Rome, Madrid and Athens, Cesar and Napoleon, and took a long time to acknowledge that they lived in the equinoctial regions of Colombia, near jungles of anacondas and tropical seas with singing whales.

At that time Antioquia did not extend to the Caribbean coast, since Urabá and Darién, the lands explored by Balboa, belonged to the vast and heterogeneous state of el Cauca. It was in those two zones that the earliest mainland colonization took place during the Conquest – the site of the legendary city of Santa María la Antigua del Darién, the first mainland settlement in the Americas; the town where, at the beginning of the 16th Century, Gonzalo Fernández de Oviedo wrote, in a house surrounded by lemon trees, the first and perhaps the last novel of chivalry that would be written in America; and the point where the Atrato flows into the sea, the river with the fastest flow in the world.

Next came the state of Cundinamarca, centered round the savanna of Bogotá and the city that presided over the changing fortunes of the country since colonial times. Where the two legislative Houses made laws and orators deployed their eloquence, where politics was in the hands of grammarians and party bosses, where powerful politicians invented a style that would later proliferate throughout the whole country.

The seventh state stretched over the immense savanna to the lands of Boyacá, on whose hills decisive battles were fought in the War of Independence, and where the Colony seems to peacefully persist in villages with an austere and simple look, pleasant wheat-fields and valleys full of sheep; on the dry and stony plains of Villa de Leyva; and in sleepy Tunja, with its baroque oratories and magnificent chapels, enormous central plaza, great cathedral and the ceremonial stones where the solar rituals of the ancient Chibcha Indians were carried out for centuries.

The eighth state was el Tolima, which spread in the south from the sources of the river Magdalena, where a site full of enormous stone statues of the gods – jaguars and eagles of enigmatic design – marks the legacy of one of the earliest indigenous civilizations, and carried on northwards through the valley of the Magdalena and the Central Cordillera, in what are today the departments of el Huila and el Tolima. A zone of great snow-covered mountains and volcanoes: el Huila, el Tolima, Santa Isabel and el Ruiz, whose eruptions over the ages covered the land with clouds of ash that fertilized the valleys and high savannas, and in times of thaw, caused avalanches that opened great canyons. This was the region of the great indigenous gold-workers, the Tolimas; of the warlike Pijaos who were exterminated by the conquistadors, as were the Gualíes who occupied the territory to the north, where the old colonial cities of Honda and San Sebastián de Mariquita were founded. The latter was one of the republic's earliest capitals and a seat of the Botanical Expedition and its colonial hermitage displays a figure of Christ that presided over the flagship of don Juan of Austria at the battle of Lepanto.

Finally, there was the state of el Cauca, which at that time covered all the peripheral regions that were practically unknown: the Chocó, with its rain forests and Pacific coastline; the canyons of the Dagua that descended towards the Valle del Cauca; what is now the department of el Cauca itself, with its coastal clearings and dark mountains, where

Opposite: Santo Domingo River. La Macarena range, Meta.

Pages 204-205: Coffee farm. Caldas.

Popayán is the city where you most clearly see the three races of which we are composed. It is a Spanish-style urban center where you nevertheless increasingly note the presence of the colorfully-dressed Guambiano and Paéz Indians. A city with a fierce statue of the conquistador who founded it on its highest hill, proud of its peaceful ridges, magnificent churches, immense houses with stone-paved courtyards and colonnades, and the enormous home of its heraldic poet Guillermo Valencia – a city torn between being the center of a seignorial world and its more ancient condition as the center of an indigenous, black and mulatto world, and recently discovering its closeness to the sea.

there were great haciendas with thousands of slaves, and still farther to the south, the region of Nariño, once the distant, northern frontier of the Inca empire, now a great patchwork quilt of smallholdings where you find energetic indigenous communities.

That nebulous state also included both the Amazon, covering what are now the departments of Putumayo, Caquetá, Vaupés and Amazonas, and the Orinoco, now the departments of el Vichada, Guainía, Arauca and Meta. In these lands, where many native communities still remain, an intricate network of rivers flow into the mighty Amazon. But these regions are now torn between the plenitude of an exuberant but fragile nature, and the sometimes devastating dynamics of world trade, intensive agriculture, cattle-farming and the illegal commerce of narcotics and wildlife.

These original states managed to stamp the character of their inhabitants with a distinctive face. Even today, it may be said that six of those large regions – the Caribbean, Antioquia, Santander, the Savanna, Tolima and the Valle del Cauca – conserve the six most distinctive ways of speaking the Spanish language that you find in Colombia, though there are nuances that distinguish the pronunciation of a person, say, from Valledupar from that of someone from Montería. From the Rionegro Constitution of 1863 till the centralist Constitution of 1886, Colombia was divided into those great federated states. They were true territorial units, distinguished by their characteristic manner of speech: the "paisa", "costeña", "santandereana", "sabanera" and "tolimense".

These five states formed the central zone of the country: the economically-active coast, both for its agriculture and cattle-farming, and its commerce; the coffee region, on which our economy depended for many decades; the mining and oil regions; the region of the sugar mills; and the regions where the major earners were, successively, *quina* bark, tobacco and sugar cane until the advent of industrialization. The whole of the formal, conventional economy was there, but it revolved, above all, around the small coffee plantations, which produced a mild coffee that became the most famous in the world. The other state, el Cauca, covered half of the country, that nearly invisible half which was not, strictly speaking, recognized by the 1886 Constitution either.

That Constitution restored centralism, the idea of a unitary country, but it wiped out the country's diversity, to our cost. A century later those neglected regions turned into a hotbed of political conflicts. They were the home of many indigenous peoples, many children of Africa, regions with unexplored riches and a great biodiversity. There fell back on them many of the peasant-farmers who had been displaced by the violence: those who wanted to continue being farmers, those who refused to become marginal inhabitants of the cities, those who did not want to be beggars or criminals – the fate imposed on them by a country that had abandoned agriculture, considering it to be somewhat archaic, but was unable to complement it with industrialization and foolishly believed, instead, in an industrialization done behind the back of the countryside, in the insane idea of an urbanization without productivity.

Opposite: La Ermita Church.
Popayán, Cauca.

Pages 208-209: El Tolima snow-covered mountain. Tolima.

Te, Candela, decet caput ex ornato Cyparis.

Ad D. Nicolaum Candela.
Ut Sol, Candela, nos flammis efficis â
Luce tua illuminas, fervonq; rudis.

- Omnis homo est albus.
- Nullus homo est albus.
- Aliquis homo est albus.
- Aliquis homo non est albus.
- Petrus est albus.
- Petrus non est albus.

Contrariæ · Subalternæ · Contradictoriæ · Subcontrariæ · Subalternæ

Discipulus certe verq; in ullasque Minava
Et tua mente[qu]a manent, eripis inscitias.

Dictatore Patre — Joseph — Nicolao Candela

Auditore Dominico Osorio anno 1747.

INHABITING THE LANGUAGE

Nowadays, when Colombia is becoming visible to the eyes of the world, after centuries of invisibility, many people are going to wonder why this country where all of the crises of the early 21st century converge is so strange, and they will thus turn to the writers and artists who interpreted the reality of Colombia over the centuries and find, in that reality, the exceptional historical case of a country which began to modernize itself and became one of the first to witness the collapse of the paradigms of modernity.

The search for a correct use of language was always one of the greatest anxieties of Colombians. We owe to it our vague renown for speaking the best Spanish on the continent, a reputation that reveals, instead, the long persistence of the colonial model, an enormous resistance to the incorporation of original contributions, an obsession with the worship of the metropolis and the enthronement of the purebred as an irrevocable canon. What is obvious is that from the very beginning, marking every one of the great historical moments of our society, literature was always present, providing a testimony to events, forging our symbols and nourishing the renovation of our language.

At the time of the Conquest, as we have seen, Colombia saw the birth of the impressive and meticulous naturalist epic poem *Elegías de varones ilustres de Indias*, by Juan de Castellanos, a splendid poetic synthesis of 16th century America and the earliest attempt to create a linguistic *mestizaje*. A legion of clear and observant chroniclers set out to capture, in language and memory, the essence of that age of marvels and atrocities, from the first great historian of America, Gonzalo Fernández de Oviedo, "regidor" (alderman) of Santa María la Antigua del Darién to fray (friar) Pedro Simón, who collected diverse testimonies which later formed the basis of his detailed account of the birth of an epoch, and including Cieza de León, who began to write his chronicle in Cartago and finished it in Peru.

Later, during the Colony, our culture expressed itself in Hernando Domínguez's *Poema heroico a san Ignacio de Loyola* (heroic poem in honor of St. Ignatius of Loyola), which followed in the footsteps of *culteranismo*, but, exploring baroque resources, combined the expressiveness of the Spanish language with the exuberance of American lands. After that there was the mystical exercise of mother Francisca Josefa del Castillo, who came, on these cold savannas so far from Saint Teresa and el Escorial, to experience visions, voices, prodigies, trances and transfixions comparable to those which had been felt by the Spanish mystics. Such was the extent to which there were transferred to our lands not only the religious ornaments of that late Middle Ages that Spain was going through at the time but also the corresponding mental states.

There were many writers during the colonial period: above all, we should not forget Francisco Álvarez de Velasco y Zorrilla, governor of Neiva and author of numerous verbal mazes and contrivances, who was a highly typical representative of an epoch when the curiosity and the spirit of adventure which had formerly expressed itself in everyday life and exploration decayed and people found refuge in language. Later on, in the time of the Independence, appeared the brief but charming work of Luis Vargas Tejada, a

Opposite:
P. Nicolao Candela, *Cursus Philosophicus*. R., illuminated manuscript, 1747, Historical Archive of el Colegio Mayor de Nuestra Señora del Rosario. Bogotá.

Pages 212-213:
Billboard. Bogotá.

young humanist whose passion for politics prevented him from achieving artistic maturity and fulfillment. He had written the marvelous one-act farce, *Las convulsiones*, inspired by an Italian piece, but full of an original use of language, a text that still conserves the freshness and wit of an unmistakably Creole spirit:

> If they are merchants: what hardship
> going up and down the Magdalena!
> Enduring the mosquitoes and the rowers:
> Here caught by the caiman, there drowned,
> attacked by tertian fevers somewhere else,
> the rowers abandoned you and went off,
> the pilot insults and plunders you,
> a mayor harasses and humiliates you;
> and when you reach the port from the sea,
> you're already desperate and half dead.
> You don't get much rest in Cartagena,
> boiling in the heat, stepping on the sand,
> living in a shack like a cat,
> drinking water that tastes like the sole of a shoe,
> putting up with the customs officials,
> but a week would not be sufficient
> if I were to set forth for you
> all that the poor merchant suffers…

La Pedrera, Caquetá.

The mestizo peoples, now inscribed in the schemes of history, can only renounce historical memory at the cost of living in the world in a makeshift way. They wind up turning the exuberance of nature into their poverty, its fecundity into their tragedy and its wealth into their curse.

But after that, Vargas became the main instigator of the plot against Bolívar. When it failed, he had to flee Bogotá and hide in a cavern on the road to Casanare, where, a year later, trying to escape to Venezuela, he was carried away by the raging waters as he tried to cross a flooded river of the prairies.

Nowadays, when Colombia is becoming visible to the eyes of the world, after centuries of invisibility, many people are going to wonder why this country where all of the crises of the early 21st century converge is so strange, and they will thus turn to the writers and artists who interpreted the reality of Colombia over the centuries and find, in that reality, the exceptional historical case of a country which began to modernize itself and became one of the first to witness the collapse of the paradigms of modernity.

In a region condemned to a peripheral, second-hand position in philosophical terms, abnormality in scientific terms and irrationality in philosophical terms, only the creative imagination was able to grapple with this reality, which seemed too absurd to be interpreted through concepts and too unstable to be organized into institutions.

For those who expound a theory of historical norms, for those who still believe that there are invariable laws that rule what happens to nations – that the development of

216 Carmelo Fernández, *White and Indian racial type*, 1851, watercolor. Chorographic Commission. National Library of Colombia.

their societies inevitably follows a recognizable succession of periods and stages– Colombia must represent an extreme case of abnormality, an embodiment of the absurd.

All of Latin America is like that, but insofar as the other countries are a little more homogeneous it is possible that they show a greater social coherence, a greater precision in their historical processes. Here, every unifying discourse always seemed like a mask put on to disguise our complexity, an attempt at simplification. The very rigidity of our language, its attachment to the sources and origins, its subjection to the authority of the academies, was a formal effort, by the elites and the most traditionalist sectors of society, to avoid being sucked into the whirlpool of diversity.

Perhaps it was for this reason that Colombian poetry never wholly surrendered to the avant-garde adventures that intoxicated, in equal measure, the countries that are mostly European, like Argentina and Chile; mostly indigenous, like Mexico and Peru; and mostly Afro-American, like Cuba. While Huidobro was writing in Chile and Vallejo in Peru, while Tablada and Paz were experimenting in Mexico and the poetic entanglements of José Lezama Lima proliferated in Cuba, Colombia persisted in following the guidelines of Quevedo and Rubén Darío, and instead of doing capers in the air emphasized their tonalities.

Barba Jacob heightened their tone of agony and pathos, Valencia carried their marmoreal harmonies to an extreme, geniality and refined grace abounded in the poetry of Luis Carlos López and the symphonic work of León de Greiff brought an extreme virtuosity to the melodic experiments of Darío.

This is not to say the poetic excess that flourished elsewhere was wanting here, but it is only fair to point out that in Colombia such excess was more a matter of abundance, fullness and unruliness than an intellectual twisting of meaning.

Perhaps our reality was already too confused, too torrential and bewildering, for there to be a need to deliberately make it more complex and obscure. Faithful to the patriarchs of old, Castellanos and Domínguez Camargo, or faithful to the reality that gave birth to those founding fathers, Colombian poets tended to be excessive, but they knew how to weave delicate harmonies in the margins of that excess. Rubén Darío had written this condemnation of fatherhood to his son:

> Slow to come is this pain to which you come,
> to this horrible world of sorrow and terror,
> dream 'neath the angels, sleep 'neath the saints,
> you'll soon have a whole life to be poisoned by.

Barba Jacob takes this sentiment to an extreme:

> Despite all, Cynthia of mine, in the frozen night
> next to my livid flesh your rosy flesh
> and may a child slash the olden mists of the path.

Nevertheless, it is surprising to find in Carlyle's Sartor Resartus, *that kind of world history of clothing, that when the philosopher tries to describe the most austere dress that mankind has ever invented, he does not choose the* chlamys *of Ancient Greece or Roman toga or Gypsy* pareo *or African cloaks, but the single garment worn over the shoulders by the ragged and practically naked soldiers of the Liberator Simón Bolívar in the mortally cold high moors of the Andes: a square of cloth with a straight slit in the center. Thus it was that, in Carlyle's book, the abstract idea of the poncho and its Colombian equivalent, the* ruana, *possibly owed to the refined sense of design of the continent's Indians, won the honor of being declared the greatest example of sobriety in human dress.*

> If it is a crime to give new shoots to dark matter,
> I will purge in myself the erotic madness
> of two sad wolf cubs that were suckled by fate.

Barba Jacob is the most sublime poet of Colombia, not in the sense that he has written the most impeccable work, but in the sense that scattered throughout his turbulent, fitful and uneven work are to be found the most powerful verses in our poetry and some of the most powerful in the Spanish language. It is also true in the sense that no one examined the enigmas of Colombia and interpreted our mental and emotional agonies as he did. Valéry said that many architects never knew that they were only building palaces so that posterity would be able to marvel at the few exquisite porticoes that survived their ruin. For many, reading the whole of *Acuarimántima* may be wearisome, for the poem is weak and hyperbolic at times, but its verses are full of miracles and even the weak or wordy ones set the spirit up for the sudden surprises:

> Nothing, nothing forever, and my soul,
> cheated by the gods, was deserving
> of truth and loyalty and harmony.
> Be worthy of this horror and this nothingness
> and energetic and brave, oh soul of mine!

Some verses of Barba Jacob seem to summarize our current dilemmas, plumbing our deepest concerns and oldest limitations. For example, Barba Jacob, loyal to a centenary tradition of bloody conflict, winds up uttering this grievous cry, which no longer expresses a rebellion against reality but a mistrust of language.

> Peace is my violent enemy
> And love is my bloodthirsty enemy

None of our poets so strongly confronted the theme of self-hatred, of despising who we are, to the point of assuming it as his own drama; he also warned of the danger it implied:

> I despise myself, I am full of sores,
> I despise myself, you have gangrened
> my heart.

In Valencia, by contrast, we find an exquisite tracing, a well-worked elaboration, a sense of balance and in the midst of such correctness, sudden brushes with mystery and with the arcane:

Opposite: "Yipaos" (jeeps), cars used for passengers and freight in the coffee zone. Armenia, Quindío.

Pages 220-221: Mavecure ridges. Guanía.

For those who expound a theory of historical norms, for those who still believe that there are invariable laws that rule what happens to nations –that the development of their societies inevitably follows a recognizable succession of periods and stages– Colombia must represent an extreme case of abnormality, an embodiment of the absurd.

, se volvió a
 sonreía con deseo
 hacerle algún reproche que
 no salía de la vieja boca desdentada.
—Nooo, sí, a mí no me gusta eso, res
pondió, como para librarse de una vez
por todas del peso de su falta. Le parecía
que al confesarla todo quedaba resuelto
y que más grave que el hecho mismo
era la forma que tomaba al relatár
lo.
—¿Ya comió sumercé?
—Pero dónde?

si qued
lató 7

> They are sons of the desert, the palm tree lent them
> a long mobile neck which feigns its swaying,
> and into their withered rostrums which the chimera sculpts
> the mouth of the sphinx blew eternal weariness.

It is impossible not to be moved when you hear him say things that we only half understand, like:

> Drink sorrow in them, flautists of Byzantium.

Or when we feel again the timelessness of profoundly moving verses:

> That I loved you peerlessly, you knew
> and the Lord knows it; never does the wandering ivy
> cling to the friendly grove
> as your being joined to my sad soul.

But also in prose this audacity and effectiveness was seen from the start and our prose likewise inclined less to experiments with form than to classical correctness. Tomás Carrasquilla, that meticulous observer of reality, deploys a language that is rich and quite expressive, but deliberately limited to registering the sonority and mentality of his region. José Eustasio Rivera always subordinates his syntactic experiments to the need to convey the atmosphere of the jungle regions that he describes, so that his innovations, like those of the Chroniclers of the Indies, do not arise from a literary zeal, from the wish to explore the possibilities of language, but from the need to use language to make the reader aware of things that are not in the language but in an unnamed world which the author wishes to share.

Once, in his typically provocative way, Jorge Luis Borges asked why humor was such a persistent recourse in Colombian life. The Argentinean poet recalled how, one time, while on an outing in a park in Bogotá with a professor from the University of the Andes, he wanted to know the name of the person commemorated by a statue standing amidst the trees. "It must be some notable man, because in this country there are many notable men and very few heroes". "No Argentinean would have said that," Borges explained, pointing out that such irreverence towards all that is respectable is something that is typically Colombian. We might say that the battle against the shameful powers that be, which have been never been politically defeated in Colombia, has been waged in a very curious way in the field of language, and one characteristic of the restless and untamed spirit of this society is its verbal independence, a wariness of any attempt at imposition by the person you dialogue with, distrust, reticence and the inability to speak, intellectually, with innocence.

Original manuscripts of *La cuarta batería*, a novel by Eduardo Zalamea Borda.

There is no doubt that in Colombia language has been an instrument of defense against power, of a struggle against an officially-imposed forgetfulness, but it is also a mechanism which Colombians spontaneously employ to adapt themselves to the world, and even at times, to shrug their shoulders at it. Tracking down the forms of popular speech in Colombia would be an arduous job.

Fernando Botero, *Man on horseback*, sculpture. Renacimiento Park. Bogotá. The shrine of Monserrate is in the background.

Here, every unifying discourse always seemed like a mask put on to disguise our complexity, an attempt at simplification. The very rigidity of our language, its attachment to the sources and origins, its subjection to the authority of the academies, was a formal effort, by the elites and the most traditionalist sectors of society, to avoid being sucked into the whirlpool of diversity.

Valencia speaks somewhere of someone who is willing to sacrifice a world in order to polish a verse. It is also possible that a Colombian would be capable of sacrificing all of it to polish a jest and it is curious to find an ambiguous conduct in poets like José Asunción Silva, whose lyric work is sobbing and solemn, but also wrote *Gotas amargas* (Bitter Pills), ironic and mischievous poems that might have been inspired by Heine.

His life, full of grievous episodes that finally led him to suicide, also abounds in amusing incidents. In fact, Silva was a great imitator of voices and personages, a scoffer who devoted his life to commerce and who alternated melancholy and dandyism, like Baudelaire. We may say of Barba Jacob as well, that when we read his poetry, we find ourselves before an impassioned, grave and poignant man, but when we read his biography there appears, instead, a man given to impudent remarks and humorous pranks. There is no doubt either that this ambiguity can be found, at the beginning of the republican era, in Luis Vargas Tejada, although it would be more accurate to say that his drama was seen in his life, and his humor in his verses. Another poet who went through these contrasting moods was Rafael Pombo, the greatest 19th century one before Silva, who irrupted into literature with a great philosophical poem, *Hora de tinieblas* (Time of darkness).

After this poem, transcendentally rebellious and nearly blasphemous in places, considering the extremely narrow-minded Catholic ambit of the Bogotá of his period, Pombo gradually changed his tone so that by the end of his life, after having lived for a long time in New York, he wound up being known only for his children's fables. Nevertheless, there is an abyss between the tormented Pombo of:

Why did I come to be born,
who forces me to suffer,
who enacted this hostile law
of living in order to suffer?

and the Pombo of *Renacuajo paseador* (The tadpole he would a walking go)

The son of the frog, Rin Rin the tadpole,
went out this morning very sprightly and smart,
with short trousers, fashionable tie,
hat with a band and fancy waistcoat.
He met on his way his neighbor, a mouse,
who said: come with me, friend.
Let's visit Mrs. Mouse together
and there'll be a big spread and a feast.

The verses of this memorable and rather cruel outing by a tadpole and a little mouse make up a nursery rhyme which virtually every Colombian child learns.

226   Above: Eladio Gil, *The Indian woman Catalina*, bronze sculpture, 1974. Cartagena, Bolívar.

Below: Monument to a pair of old shoes. Bronze sculpture commemorating the famous poem about Cartagena by Luis Carlos López, also known as "el tuerto" (the one-eyed). Cartagena, Bolívar.

Pages 228-229: Barichara, Santander.

At the beginning of the 20th century, this passion for verbal witticisms, liking for improvisation and temptation to cleverness crystallized in the literary school known as the "Gruta Simbólica" (Symbolic Grotto), a group of Bogotá versifiers who were joined by some outstanding poets from others regions of the country. It is difficult to assert that they left us a finished body of work, because much of this wit and even this verbal skill was wasted on occasional stanzas and funny stories, and it might even be said that the Gruta Simbólica showed the country the limitations of a humor that was extremely parish-pump and of talents that were not put at the service of nobler causes.

The most outstanding works of the poets who participated in those literary gatherings were written on their fringes, like the poems of Carlos Villafañe, who was much better as a poet of the paradoxes of love than a lively minstrel, although his farewell to Jorge Pombo at the Bogotá Central Cemetery has the charm of a colloquial conversation while it plumbs, at the same time, the depths of a definitive goodbye and thus achieves a certain dramatic tension that is delicately inserted into the apparent triviality of the verses:

> Sheep that leaves the sheepfold
> to where the echo of my voice does not carry,
> a thousand greetings to Julio de Francisco
> and a warm embrace for Eduardo Ortega.

Colombian humor would find a much more austere and delicate outlet for personal expression and a much more effective one in social terms in the work of the Cartagena poet Luis Carlos López, who left his mark on a period of Latin American poetry. His poetry is critical and acid, like that of the contemporary to whom he may be compared, Ramón López Velarde, who knew how to love Mexico with a playful sweetness. Few in Mexico would make fun of Mexico, no one in Buenos Aires would make fun of Buenos Aires, but perhaps there is no Colombian who would not be tempted to make fun of Colombia. In *La suave patria* (The gentle fatherland), López Velarde only dares to do it to his country in a tender way:

> The Christ-child deeded you a stable
> And the devil, the veins of petroleum.

Luis Carlos López speaks of his native city, flattered by the rhetoric of nobility and heraldry, with deliberate irreverence:

> You were heroic in colonial times,
> when your sons, noble eagles,
> weren't a flock of swifts.
> But today, full of a rancid shabbiness,

Colombian humor would find a much more austere and delicate outlet for personal expression and a much more effective one in social terms in the work of the Cartagena poet Luis Carlos López, who left his mark on a period of Latin American poetry. His poetry is critical and acid, like that of the contemporary to whom he may be compared, Ramón López Velarde, who knew how to love Mexico with a playful sweetness. Few in Mexico would make fun of Mexico, no one in Buenos Aires would make fun of Buenos Aires, but perhaps there is no Colombian who would not be tempted to make fun of Colombia.

you may well inspire that affection
which one feels for a pair of old shoes.

Another of the favorite targets of Colombian humor was always the Church, whose pincers fastened on free spirits for centuries. With great skill, Luis Carlos López depicts the clerical power that governs provincial towns and draws his own mental self-portrait in the face of it:

The shadow that forms a pool
on the rural square
invites one to a soothing
Sunday rest.

Frail, in a dog collar,
crosses it, reading a missal,
the lord and master of the meek,
uncouth town, the asinine town.

Wearing a stiff cassock
of serge, he doesn't care a fig
about the poverty of the fold.

And I, from my window,
cleaning a gun, ask myself,
What should I do with this gun?

Our poets, quite capable of loving nature and even the misfortune which the country brings them, regard our institutions with scorn. In the festive and adventurous verses of the *Relato de Ramón Antigua* (Tale of Ramón Antigua) León de Grieff thus writes:

On the hill of Otramina
already within reach of el Cauca
I met up with Martín Vélez
as drunk, by God, as a lord.
I came across Toño Duque
mounted on his white mule
I met up with mister Grey
he of the reddish beard.

Antonio Samudio. *Slopes of Monserrate* (detail), 1972, acrylic on canvas. 99 x 99 cm. Suramericana de Seguros Collection.

At the beginning of the 20th century, this passion for verbal witticisms, liking for improvisation and temptation to cleverness crystallized in the literary school known as the "Gruta Simbólica" (Symbolic Grotto), a group of Bogotá versifiers who were joined by some outstanding poets from others regions of the country. It is difficult to assert that they left us a finished body of work, because much of this wit and even this verbal skill was wasted on occasional stanzas and funny stories...

232 Mundo Aventura Park. Bogotá.

Opposite: Salitre Mágico Park. Bogotá.

In a region condemned to a peripheral, second-hand position in philosophical terms, abnormality in scientific terms and irrationality in philosophical terms, only the creative imagination was able to grapple with this reality, which seemed too absurd to be interpreted through concepts and too unstable to be organized into institutions.

> The three went along tipsy
> just as the law ordains,
> defying the gods of Olympus
> with horrisonous boasts,
> insolent cries,
> bewildered thoughts,
> tipsy the three went along
> and with three sprees riding pillion,
> that is to say, a reserve
> of bottles in the rear…

It ends with this fine description of life in the tropics:

> They went down to the passage,
> climbed into the hammocks,
> now came the reckoning
> of the day's affairs.
>
> While the grub is served
> you boisterously talk,
> while you talk, you smoke,
> you drink while you dine,
> you utter an exaggerated
> stew of near lies,
> while the pot sings on the stove,
> while the mountain dreams,
> a dream of robust ceibo-trees
> and of very slender palms…

But as soon as he turns to the official country his tone changes:

> All that verbiage-stuffed rabble,
> fairground rogues, geese of the Capitol,
> ruffians, Abderites, claims-jumpers,
> inferior caste whose glands have been robbed of their juice,
> inferior caste given the eloquence of impotency,
> they cause me loathing, they make me queasy, they provoke my hysterical laughter.
> And, I, Gaspar, I'm off – with the knapsack of my scorn,
> with every right, logically – towards the absurd.

Rodeolandia Park. Bogotá.

Barba Jacob is the most sublime poet of Colombia, not in the sense that he has written the most impeccable work, but in the sense that scattered throughout his turbulent, fitful and uneven work are to be found the most powerful verses in our poetry and some of the most powerful in the Spanish language. It is also true in the sense that no one examined the enigmas of Colombia and interpreted our mental and emotional agonies as he did.

And in another part he wants to flee:

Far from the Santanders and Bolívars.

Another great social critic, full of erudition and charm, is Hernando Martínez Rueda, (with the penname "Martinón"), an outstanding poet in the ambit of his time, whose verses are much more than a matter of fortunate witticisms, because they deploy a profound irony and powerful critical capacity. For example, his "Song of the future imperfect", which traces a parallel between the republican oratory of the politicians and their style of governing:

Colombia is the country of the future, a tropical Eden.
With bowels of oil, valleys of sugar, mountains of salt.

Syria has not more balsam, Golconda more gold, Ophir more pearls
(That check may be ready for you at mid-year).

Its rivers flow like Niles, two seas embrace the fertile land.
(Madam, maybe we'll send you the gas in a month).

We have been given the heron of pink down, the tortoise of golden shell.
(Your little matter is going to take some time, they still haven't passed the law).

You can pluck more emeralds from the rocks than cedars from the forest.
(The honorable secretary is away, you can wait for him, if you like).

The air is filled with everything from the giant condor to the delicate hummingbird.
(Come back on Monday to make your statement, if the judge is here).

The prairie is barely sufficient for the cattle, the branch for the fruit, the waters for the fish.
(Perhaps you can inquire again next week).

The soil nourishes everything from the Phoenician date to the classical grapevine.
(The document hasn't been signed, señor Cadavid is sick).

Of Colombia's future no one may have a doubt:
The future is present in Colombia: it's called "to wait".

In a frank mockery of the bombastic "Day of the Race" which has been celebrated in Colombia since the arrival of the white man, the Pereira poet Luis Carlos González,

236 Afro-Colombian fruit vendor. Cartagena, Bolívar.

We should remember that in Colombia political and cultural domination always made use of the language. From the beginning language was meant to betray who was or was not a Spaniard; who belonged to the ruling classes and who came from the people; who had phonetic difficulties because of his roots in the defeated languages; who spoke Spanish with a Chibcha, Emberá or Angolan coast accent.

author of very popular patriotic songs in the *bambuco* genre, like *La ruana* (the ruana is the Colombian poncho) and *Mi casta* (My race), wrote those famous verses which do not scorn insolence but have the virtue of giving the frequent insults a sociological content:

> A race of hidalgos? No, a race of party bosses,
> a realm of blunderbusses and liquor stills
> on a barren backyard of cowardice,
> from whose past, the one which our ancestors scrutinize,
> only the whoreson survives,
> And we are still denying it.

Borges believed that it was the marginal position of the Jews which enabled them to have such importance in European culture and that an analogous marginality was responsible for the strength and grandeur of the Irish in English literature. It would difficult to find sharper pens than those of Swift, Bernard Shaw, James Joyce and Oscar Wilde. There is no doubt that in Colombia language has been an instrument of defense against power, of a struggle against an officially-imposed forgetfulness, but it is also a mechanism which Colombians spontaneously employ to adapt themselves to the world, and even at times, to shrug their shoulders at it.

If anything characterizes the urbanization of our customs, it is a notable hostility towards the past and the simplicity of the peasant-farmer, the superstitious incorporation of a supposed modernity into the language and a persistent effort to deny our origins. From the beginning language was meant to betray who was or was not a Spaniard; who belonged to the ruling classes and who came from the people; who had phonetic difficulties because of his roots in the defeated languages; who spoke Spanish with a Chibcha, Emberá or Angolan coast accent. In the central regions and in the official culture of Colombia speaking in a purebred way became an obsession, although certain differences were established from the beginning.

We do not know in what moment the Spanish pronunciation of the *zeta*, which is different from the *ese*, was definitively relinquished, but it probably reflected Creole resistance, although it may also have been the result of the primacy of the Andalusians in the forming of the Latin American language. A Spanish pronunciation might even have been dangerous in an ambit of pro-Independence sentiments.

Another form that died out in America was the orthodox second person plural, although children are still often taught the orthodox Spanish scheme at school, in which the personal pronouns are: *Yo, tú, él, nosotros, vosotros, ellos*. It seems poor taste to enumerate the personal pronouns in the following way: *Yo, usted, él, nosotros, ustedes, ellos*; although that is how they are used in real life in many places. Even those who have restored the use of the archaic and ceremonial *vos*, transferred to the singular, like the Argentineans

Bay of Taganga, Magdalena.

Valencia speaks somewhere of someone who is willing to sacrifice a world in order to polish a verse. It is also possible that a Colombian would be capable of sacrificing all of it to polish a jest and it is curious to find an ambiguous conduct in poets like José Asunción Silva, whose lyric work is sobbing and solemn, but also wrote Gotas amargas *(Bitter Pills), ironic and mischievous poems that might have been inspired by Heine.*

240   El Cocuy, Boyacá.

Some verses of Barba Jacob seem to summarize our current dilemmas, plumbing our deepest concerns and oldest limitations. For example, Barba Jacob, loyal to a centenary tradition of bloody conflict, winds up uttering this grievous cry, which no longer expresses a rebellion against reality but a mistrust of language:

*Peace is my violent enemy
And love is my
bloodthirsty enemy.*

and the people of Antioquia and the Valle del Cauca, do not extend it to the plural and normally, they conjugate: *yo, vos, él, nosotros, ustedes, ellos*. But it is with the second person that you enter into debate and it would seem that this was the point at which the desire for independence was defined. To address the Spanish as *vosotros* was probably regarded as the equivalent of continuing to feel that we were still Spanish ourselves, and so the hidden genius of *mestizaje* invented this distancing formula, which today marks a fundamental difference between our worlds.

Below: Cachipay, Cundinamarca.

Pages 242-243: Concert hall of the Jorge Tadeo Lozano University. Bogotá.

IN SEARCH OF COLOMBIA

Most of us, in Colombia, have heard all our lives of legendary lands within our country that we have never visited. For the average inhabitant of the Atlantic coast, and even of the interior of the country, the Amazon jungle is an inaccessible fabrication. For someone from Bogotá or Cali, a journey to the Atlantic coast is one of the great adventures of life. Colombia is a big country, but there is something much more crucial than mileage which makes the distances seem so great and that is the diversity of the territory.

There is a song by Carlos Huertas in which one man from the Caribbean region addresses another and, with great courtesy, says that the song the latter sings is very nice but that it does not tell him where the song is from. All he knows is that it is not from Valledupar, nor the region of the Magdalena, nor from Bolívar, the northern department whose capital is Cartagena.

> Well, I have the feeling that your songs
> are from an unknown land.

But the man who is thus addressed is not from some region distant from the Colombian Caribbean: he is not from the savanna of Bogotá or the Pacific coast or the blue mountains of el Huila, nor the remote jungles of the Putumayo: his unknown land is right there, in the center of a neighboring region:

> With great pleasure and great pride
> I am from the middle of the Guajira
> – the man says –
> I was born in Dibulla, facing the Caribbean
> when I was little, they took me away from there,
> Barrancas was where I was baptized,
> and in the whole of the Guajira I became free.

It seems archaic, this idea that a neighboring department is felt to be so distant, but in the work of García Márquez too it is easy to see that we are dealing with a territory in which a short journey in any direction leads men into unknown lands. For the inhabitants of Macondo, enclosed in a magical hamlet on the banks of a nameless river, all of the neighboring lands are a mystery. The explorers search in vain for the sea, which is only a few leagues away, however, and only encounter a vestige of it in the form of a fantastic galleon on solid land, covered in tropical vegetation. The nearby stretch of marshes only seems to lead to never-never land and to get the mules which carry the mail to communicate with the rest of the territory and the distant capital of the republic is a major challenge. In his memoirs García Márquez also recalls, as legendary journeys, the expeditions made by his parents through the foothills of the

Opposite: Olga de Amaral, *Orión Umbra 44* (detail), 2004, canvas, gesso and gold leaf. 70 x 300 cm. Casa de Nariño (Presidential Palace). Bogotá.

Pages 246-247: Sierra Nevada de Santa Marta, Magdalena.

Sierra Nevada, which separates the prairies of el Cesar from the desert regions of la Guajira, a land of dust clouds that stretch out, as he says in another passage, "beneath the mercurial light of those wastes of salt".

Most of us, in Colombia, have heard all our lives of legendary lands within our country that we have never visited. For the average inhabitant of the Atlantic coast, and even of the interior of the country, the Amazon jungle is an inaccessible fabrication. For someone from Bogotá or Cali, a journey to the Atlantic coast is one of the great adventures of life. Colombia is a big country, but there is something much more crucial than mileage which makes the distances seem so great and that is the diversity of the territory. To go from Manizales to Honda, for example, only takes three hours by car. Nevertheless, to travel those three hours not only implies crossing dizzying precipices, high moors, dark abysses and mist-covered gorges, but also pretty, flowery landscapes in a temperate climate with pleasant hills divided by green rivers, and going from a cold, misty terrain of dark vegetation to a hot valley full of hills wrought into fantastic shapes by the drought.

The journey from Cali to Buenaventura doesn't take more than three hours either, but what a wealth of landscapes stretch out! From the exceptionally fertile valley of the Cauca, crossing the canyons of the Dagua and the cliffs of the Western Cordillera, to reach those flooded lands of the coastal jungles: from the region of palms to the tangled mangrove swamps on the seashore. When you are in Cali, a city screened off from the sea by the rocky cliffs, the verses of the following song, so often heard, evoke places that seem remote:

> Beautiful sea port, my Buenaventura,
> where you always breathe the pure breeze.

Even more difficult is to remember, in Popayán or Pasto, that those departments are coastal ones, that very close to those cold, Andean cities, so colonial and Catholic, you catch the fiery breath of ocean storms, see the steam rising from the exquisite banquets prepared by the Blacks of Guapi and hear the sweet songs of the women who catch piangua clams in Tumaco

In the songs of Rafael Escalona, too, you note that curious sensation of a country that is full of secrets and enormous distances for its inhabitants. Although, in the following song, one reason for the alienation of travel is having to leave behind a loved one, we cannot help feeling that the journey between two places that are so near is described as an odyssey:

> I go through Valencia,
> Pass by la Sabana,
> Caracolicito

University of Cauca and Santo Domingo Church. Popayán, Cauca.

Even more difficult is to remember, in Popayán or Pasto, that those departments are coastal ones, that very close to those cold, Andean cities, so colonial and Catholic, you catch the fiery breath of ocean storms, see the steam rising from the exquisite banquets prepared by the Blacks of Guapi and hear the sweet songs of the women who catch piangua clams in Tumaco.

Opposite: The snow-covered mountain of el Ruiz, seen from the city of Manizales. Caldas.

Prairies of el Caraparo.

Despite all the technological advances, it was more difficult to travel through the country at the end of the 20th century or the middle or beginning of it than in colonial times. Today there are very few Colombians who are able to experience a continental destiny, experiences like those which the conquistadors or men of the Independence went through.

> And then to Fundación…
> And well, then
> I have to get on
> a demon,
> a devil that they call a train,
> which chugs off,
> and through the whole zone passes,
> and at evening
> goes into Santa Marta.

Opposite: Metro station. Medellín.

Pages 254-255: Eastern prairies.

I remember having told a Frenchwoman I know that once, to go from Fresno, in northern Tolima to visit a friend of my father who had his hacienda in the valley of the Magdalena, we traveled by car to la Dorada, then did a stretch by *autoferro* (a converted bus that runs on rails), then embarked in canoes along the river Ermitaño, which was full of treacherous logs, and finally got on some horses that awaited us for the final stage of the journey. My friend immediately wrote in her diary: "four means of locomotion to visit a single friend".

When we read about Bolívar's journey along the Magdalena, in the novel *El general en su laberinto* (The general in his labyrinth) or Jose Asunción Silva's, along the same river on his way to Cartagena, as related in Fernando Vallejo's book *Chapolas negras* (Butterflies of ill omen), the same alienation appears to us: the variety of the landscape and the difficulties of travel, the change of climates and customs, the strange sensation of having set out for distant lands. This is not different from the way that Jorge Isaacs arranges his narrative in the novel *María*, where he devotes much less space to Efraín's voyage from London to Buenaventura than to his journey from Buenaventura to Cali, where every boulder in the canyon of the Dagua and every river he crosses becomes an obstacle that is tough to surmount. In José Eustasio Rivera's *La vorágine* (The Vortex), a veritable apotheosis of the difficulties of the physical terrain, we feel, from the outset, the gravitational pull of that enigmatic and menacing thing represented by the word "Casanare". Beyond the Casanare is the jungle, and, awaiting us, at the far edge of the novel, is that fatal final sentence, which symbolizes so many things about our relationship with the land: "Not a sign of them: the jungle swallowed them up".

Of course, times have changed. And I would not say that Colombia is impassable. You have only to recall with what excitement and delight Humboldt traversed it two centuries ago and numerous travelers and expeditionaries have done it since What I would say is that it always seemed that living in this country required individuals to belong to one region and feel others to be alien. I would say that for some factor that has to do with the structure and complexity of our territory, it is difficult to be a Colombian, it is difficult to see the country as a whole and feel that you belong to the whole of it, and perhaps a proof of it is the ease with which we Colombians periodi-

Opposite: Vaults of the San Felipe Castle. Cartagena, Bolívar.

Pages 258-259: Ridges of San Martín. Casanare.

cally lose hold of our territory. Despite all the technological advances, it was more difficult to travel through the country at the end of the 20th century or the middle or beginning of it than in colonial times. Today there are very few Colombians who are able to experience a continental destiny, experiences like those which the conquistadors or men of the Independence went through.

This difficulty is not only due to the fact that Colombia is a country of regions, but also that the country is surpassed by the components of which it is made. The north belongs to a vaster region: the Caribbean, a sea and culture that unite many nations. The west belongs to something even broader: the Pacific basin; the central part, to the Andean world; the east, to the immense region of the Orinoco which also covers the Venezuelan prairies. And the south, to the complex universe of the Amazonian region. You might say that the only way to understand Colombia is to not limit yourself to looking at it from within its frontiers. It is a border country that belongs to different worlds. You have to understand the continent to understand it and this is a key to its makeup, since the solution to its problems also requires you to look at them from a continental perspective or one that is even broader than a merely continental one.

It is not surprising to hear anthropologists say that Cartagena de Indias and Santiago de Cuba are sister cities, that the statue that is worshipped in their respective shrines – that of the Cathedral of the Virgin (or Lady) of Charity, surnamed "El Cobre" because her sanctuary was built in the town of that name, and the Virgin of la Candelaria in the Shrine of la Popa in Cartagena – are not only similar but that they are made out of the same maize paste. Syncretic divinities, indigenous and African, eloquent symbols of an alliance through the centuries that is not always apparent at first sight. For that reason, the Cuban independence leader Maceo's link with the Atlantic coast of Colombia is not an accident, nor is García Márquez's commitment to the Cuban revolution. Nor was it by chance that Rubén Darío's passage through Cartagena and his decision to visit president Rafael Núñez at his home in El Cabrero enabled the poet to be appointed Colombian consul in Buenos Aires, a gesture that allowed Darío to begin his cosmopolitan existence and give more depth to his decisive dialogue with the literary wealth of the continent.

For that reason as well the harp and *cuatro* (four-stringed guitar) music of the Orinoco is Colombian and Venezuelan at the same time and the Orinoco itself less a barrier than a meeting point, the center of a country of shared affinities and histories.

From the legendary smugglers of Maicao to the merchants of Cúcuta and San Antonio, the plainsmen of Arauca and the inhabitants of el Vichada, there has always been a movement towards integration that was a simple reminder of the memory of a common fatherland; the certainty that the frontiers were mere political whims, not a vocation of nations. In the same way it is difficult to decide exactly to which nation many of the indigenous peoples of the Amazon belong. The Desana, Huitotos, Tikunas, Yaguas and Kamsa belong to a world in which the frontier is an arbitrary

It is not surprising to hear anthropologists say that Cartagena de Indias and Santiago de Cuba are sister cities, that the statue that is worshipped in their respective shrines –that of the Cathedral of the Virgin (or Lady) of Charity, surnamed "El Cobre" because her sanctuary was built in the town of that name, and the Virgin of la Candelaria in the Shrine of la Popa in Cartagena– are not only similar but that they are made out of the same maize paste. Syncretic divinities, indigenous and African, eloquent symbols of an alliance through the centuries that is not always apparent at first sight.

Opposite: Casiquiare River. Meta.

Pages 262-263: Orinoco River.

… Colombia is a country that is surpassed by the components of which it is made. The north belongs to a vaster region: the Caribbean, a sea and culture that unite many nations. The west belongs to something even broader: the Pacific basin; the central part, to the Andean world; the east, to the immense region of the Orinoco which also covers the Venezuelan prairies. And the south, to the complex universe of the Amazonian region. You might say that the only way to understand Colombia is to not limit yourself to looking at it from within its frontiers…

thing: the world of the eyeless serpent, the tree of fruits, the ancestral canoe and the skin of the great anaconda.

But, as we have already noted, this complexity is not only geographical. That these tropics speak a language of Latin origin; mostly profess a religion of Jewish, Greek and Roman origin; and have been given institutions inspired by the model of the French Revolution are other factors that enrich the picture. Borges wrote that being Colombian is an act of faith. It is really difficult for Colombians to respond to the call of the nation. "For the sake of the countries of Colombia", as the beautiful verse of Aurelio Arturo has it, ceaseless wars were waged, which wound up aggravating the feeling of loss and the unawareness of roots.

Behind these civil wars that seemed to set the Colombian people against one another there was always the clash between the elite culture and the popular culture. A colonized ruling class, strongly allied with the interests of the imperialist countries, denied the popular culture's attempt to express the deeper elements of the national character and construct what might have been an admirable synthesis of Colombia out of them. In this respect, art was always a profound interpreter of reality. And we still should seek in it the keys to solving the mysteries of that reality.

An international official once said that Colombia is a country that always suffered from the curse of wealth. Gold, pearls, emeralds, timber, coffee, rubber, petroleum, bananas, coca leaves – they have not only been the great riches of the country but each has also created its own war in our land. In the 16th century, the legend of El Dorado mobilized armies of occupation that laid waste to the territory of what is now Colombia and Venezuela, searching for the real gold that would put an end to the centuries-old obsessions of the alchemists. On the coasts of Manaure, as on the island of Margarita and Cumaná in Venezuela, the Indians who lived on the shores were ruthlessly driven to extract the pearls that were sold at fabulous prices in Toledo and Augsburg. There were also periodical wars incited by those who exploited and traded the emeralds from the mines of Muzo.

Wars and more wars and with them the continual breaking of the threads of tradition, the loss of customs and of memory. And their ceaseless driving force were the political parties, which from the time of Independence handled political tensions through high-flown discourses inspired by the reality of Europe and only paid faint attention to the singularity of the world to which they belonged

At the center of the ancient two-party system of Colombia stand the figures of Bolívar and Santander. But this binary arrangement is a way of projecting Christian morality onto social deeds. Good and evil, white and black, the source of all benefits and the source of all ills, the legitimate ruler and the usurper. Anyplace in the world this bipolarity is harmful, but it is much more so in a region under the sign of the diverse, where there has always been a need for a third party to modify the arrangements, overcome prejudices and allow the new to enter in.

From the beginning this conflict between what we are and what we should be was chronic. It was perpetuated in terms of an official culture made up of shams and imperatives, and opposed to a popular culture which was not granted the same statute of privilege and respectability. The real country grew by constructing its languages on the margins and only achieved its precarious incorporation into the ambit of the dominant culture late in the day.

One of the many constants of the Colombian soul is war. Instead of head-on wars between large armies, we have seen larval (in the pathological sense) wars, devious, perverse ones; wars of kidnappings and ambushes, and from the beginning violence against the unarmed, always with the pretext that they belong to the other side; cowardly wars of the bipolar mentality against the exuberance of the plural; wars against the diversity of the country, which wind up exterminating all dissident thought, every sensibility that is different, in exactly the same way that they continually harm our natural diversity without pity.

It might be said that the greatest triumph of the Colombian establishment, which has always excluded the masses, is that it has infected its opponents with the same logic, put them to respond in the same terms, and engendered an opposition that is just as violent, silencing, intolerant and unable to accept nuances and creative alternatives.

Against the backdrop of these never-ending wars, one of the sharpest figures in Colombian mythology is the outlaw, who is not, strictly speaking, a participant in the fiesta of bipartisan war but someone who is determined to find an outlet for his personal ambition and has no other option but crime. Few countries in history would be able to show such a profusion of these rebellious types, who are not just ordinary criminals of the sort you find on the police blotter, but wind up becoming a social archetype and always, for a brief time, attain a kind of tragic celebrity when they illusorily stand out as the dominators of society.

More and more these Colombian bandits have reached the status of colorful social figures. From the solitary Efraín González, who in 1965 fought a whole army on his own in a district of Bogotá, an event that was transmitted by radio, to the great capos of the drugs trade, who gave birth to a shady slum mythology and whose example stimulated the delinquency of marginal youth. Not forgetting, of course, the fearsome brigands of the violence of the fifties, *Desquite* (Revenge) and *Sangrenegra* (Black Blood).

All were symbols of an extreme individualism: the great diversity of Colombia, combined with the irresponsibility of the State, also encouraged a great competitiveness and this led to the flourishing of a vigorous individual, hardened by rivalry and the absence of social protection. Everyone is trying to get ahead in a world that is full of obstacles and where few lend a hand. A positive consequence of this is the abundance of strong characters, intense personalities, of resourceful and talented individuals. But the individuals who grow up that way are very self-centered and if there is something which is difficult to find in Colombia, it is a discourse which ap-

Tolemaida Military Base. Melgar, Tolima.

Behind these civil wars that seemed to set the Colombian people against one another there was always the clash between the elite culture and the popular culture. A colonized ruling class, strongly allied with the interests of the imperialist countries, denied the popular culture's attempt to express the deeper elements of the national character and construct what might have been an admirable synthesis of Colombia out of them.

Opposite: Banana plantation. Magdalena.

Coffee picker. Bolombolo, Antioquia.

An international official once said that Colombia is a country that always suffered from the curse of wealth. Gold, pearls, emeralds, timber, coffee, rubber, petroleum, bananas, coca leaves – they have not only been the great riches of the country but each has also created its own war in our land.

peals to a collective effort. Everyone mistrusts the law and is unable to believe in the public good: it is difficult for such a person to consider the country's needs and join in alliances that would transform it.

Many have tried to interpret this enterprising and diabolical Colombian. One of them is found in Peralta, the protagonist of Tomas Carrasquilla's story *A la diestra de Dios padre* (On the right hand of God the father). This tale combines two very Colombian elements, religious piety and astuteness, but exceptionally joined within the framework of a great innocence. The literary types of Colombia have María as the symbol of the tempting but unattainable young woman, the enchanting creature who may only be loved as a dream, who does not allow you to come close to her in real life. This girl reappears in García Márquez, in the form of little Remedios, the grandmother who dies in near-puberty and in the disturbing image of Remedios, the Beautiful, snatched away by a miraculous wind and carried off to heaven, in body and soul, after having left a trail of men torn apart by fever and desire, or plunged into suicide.

Another awesome Colombian personage is the adventurer who gets lost in unknown territories and is devoured by the jungle. Arturo Cova, the main character of José Eustasio Rivera's novel, fulfills the destiny that seemed fated for the author, who navigated the rivers of the Orinoco, nearly lost, and penetrated the jungle, living the vulnerable life of the man who leaves the world he is accustomed to and tries to get people to look at the reality of Colombia with different eyes. A fate worthy of the Western literature of his epoch, of Franz Kafka and, above all, Joseph Conrad, in whose work man's difficult struggle with nature becomes a parable of fatality.

But perhaps there is nothing comparable to García Márquez's gallery of prototypical portraits of the Colombian soul, beginning with that grandmother Úrsula, the "mama grande" of the Atlantic coast: the hardworking, omnipresent mother who, as happens with mothers in the powerful Caribbean culture, never loses her importance. Then there are her sons: the melancholy idealist who ends up succumbing to the temptations of power, and the explosive vagabond who is only able to believe in his personal destiny and never yields to history; and her daughters, the virgin in mourning who represses her passions to an extreme, and the adoptive daughter, who never feels that she belongs to that society and in the middle of the night goes back to eating the primitive soil, losing herself in the fog of her unknown origins.

Many other, nearly emblematic, characters are to be found in García Márquez, like that magic snake oil hawker who brings a discourse and wisdom that are not incorporated into tradition, a figure who never manages to win acceptance. In *Blacamán, el bueno, vendedor de milagros* (Blacamán, the Good, Vendor of Miracles), the medicine man is also a caricature of the politician who comes to power through his tricks of magic and "dictionary rhetoric".

Opposite: La Macarena National Natural Park. Meta.

Pages 270-271: Men of the prairies. Casanare.

From the legendary smugglers of Maicao to the merchants of Cúcuta and San Antonio, the plainsmen of Arauca and the inhabitants of el Vichada, there has always been a movement towards integration that was a simple reminder of the memory of a common fatherland; the certainty that the frontiers were mere political whims, not a vocation of nations.

A CENTURY'S UPHEAVALS

Throughout the civil wars of 19th century the power of the Church and the great landowners dominated Colombia and there was no progress towards modernity, with its basic liberal reforms, lay education, civil marriage, divorce, the separation of church and state.

The exclusive protagonists of these wars were the Liberal and Conservative parties, which, from the beginning of republican life, fiercely fought each other for power, regional influence and the support of the electorate. The two parties changed their platforms in accordance with the changing times: they represented protectionism and free trade, centralism and federalism, clericalism and atheistic radicalism, the defense of slavery and abolitionism. The dynamics of these wars, however, gradually forced the two parties into a conservative defense of their respective positions. By the end of the 19th century the only apparent difference between them was that they represented two distinct sectors of the power structure.

After fifty years of Conservative hegemony, a moderate Liberalism which had already lost its anti-clerical radicalism and a good part of its vocation for social reform along the way, tried to effect a number a political reforms in the 1930's. Before the minority Conservative-party would fiercely launch itself into the reconquest of power, the Liberals themselves had already moderated their programs, abandoning the quest for a real agrarian reform in a country where a hundred families owned most of the productive land and renouncing other initiatives in the field of business, labor and the defense of natural resources.

But in the mid-1940's, the most influential politicians in both parties mounted a furious opposition to the Liberal leader, Jorge Eliécer Gaitan, who had become the most important political figure of the century and whose crusade to vindicate the rights of peasant-farmers and urban workers led Colombia, for the first time in history, to the threshold of modernity and the path to a true democracy. Gaitán knew that these countries, still marked by their colonial past, needed a movement, like the Mexican "Reform", that would incorporate the always despised people into the mythology of the nation. But the aristocrats of both parties, zealous guardians of a seigniorial tradition, were fearful of Gaitan's humble origin and his oratory, which joined the tradition of the Roman tribunes to the cries of demonstrators in the streets and electrified the masses.

All of our countries, which had inherited with the republic an order of ancient hierarchies and social aversions, had a need for these vigorous popular movements

Opposite, Mónica Meira: *Excavation*, 1999, acrylic on canvas. 120 x 120 cm.

Pages 274-275: Alejandro Obregón, *Violence* (detail), 1962, oil painting on canvas, 155 x 187 cm. Banco de la República. Bogotá.

Now, at the beginning of the 21st century, Colombia has three million displaced persons, and for the first time in its history, a massive number of exiles, a total of four million Colombians scattered throughout the world…

Opposite: Diego Mazuera, *Setting the pace* (detail), 1996, oil on canvas. 54 x 65 cm.

if their people were to decisively enter into the nation's legend, and this was the role that Gaitan and his movement seemed destined to fulfill.

But Gaitan was assassinated in April, 1948, his popular campaign was destroyed and Colombia was forced to live through the rest of the century in an ambit of intolerance and racial and class discrimination.

The most terrible expression of these conflicts between Liberals and Conservatives was the political violence of the mid-century, which greatly intensified after the murder of Gaitán. To restore its already waning influence over the people, the Conservatives, who had returned to power, unleashed an official violence against the new majorities; the political and religious leaders of both parties whipped up the fanaticism of the peasant-farmers, and terror spread through the countryside.

Its consequences were not only the massive exodus of the peasant-farmer population and the unprecedented growth of the cities, but also an aristocratic pact between Liberals and Conservatives that was known as the National Front, which briefly pacified the country but at the undemocratic cost of banning other political parties.

This process of urbanization transformed Colombia. A bucolic country of farmers turned into a licentious country of cities, where all of that enormous diversity, previously dispersed, became clearly evident. The peasant-farmers were pitched into the unfamiliar life of slums that grew and grew; and in an endless progression that no scholar understood, no politician reformed and no pious soul was able to relieve, the violent Colombianization of the cities of Colombia took place.

Slowly and confusedly, the middle classes which had had access to a good education began to search for new horizons for society. Some decades before, Jorge Isaacs – explorer, discover, anthropologist before the birth of anthropology, politician, warrior and novelist of a new world – had tried to be the clear-sighted witness to the country's complexity, and the hatred of the lettered and political quarrels had turned him, as Borges noted, into a disillusioned man. José Asunción Silva, a modernist intellectual, starry-eyed businessman, explorer of the language and renovating poet, had chosen to put a bullet into his heart in the face of the insurmountable sordidness of his world. And Barba Jacob, a peasant driven from his land by village small-mindedness, decided to flee Antioquia and Colombia in search of a wider world:

> And to wander, to wander, to wander alone,
> the light of Saturn in my temple,
> broken mast over the waves
> moving to-and-fro.

The whole history of Colombia may be seen as a history of exodus and cyclical displacement. Now, at the beginning of the 21st century, Colombia has three million displaced persons, and for the first time in its history, a massive number of exiles, a

All of our countries, which had inherited with the republic an order of ancient hierarchies and social aversions, had a need for these vigorous popular movements if their people were to decisively enter into the nation's legend, and this was the role that Gaitan and his movement seemed destined to fulfill in mid-20th century Colombia. But Gaitan was assassinated in April, 1948, his popular campaign was destroyed and Colombia was forced to live through the rest of the century in an ambit of intolerance and racial and class discrimination so hostile to the people that at times its presence was nearly imperceptible in the official history of the country.

total of four million Colombians scattered throughout the world. But we should point out that much of Colombian literature and art was created in exile, and above all in Mexico, the refuge for many of those great creators. Barba Jacob, whose name was Miguel Ángel Osorio at that time and was also known as Ricardo Arenales when he was involved in the political turmoil of Central America, lived his impassioned and turbulent destiny on a continental scale, after his escape from provincial lethargy, and he learned how to assimilate or cause to resound in his own voice the virtues of the lands that welcomed him:

> He wandered, sensual and sad, through the islands of his America,
> in a pinewood of Honduras he strengthened his spirit,
> the Mexican land gave him his rebelliousness,
> his freedom, his drive, and he was a flame in the wind.

Mexico has also been a homeland for Germán Pardo García, Gabriel García Márquez, the poet Álvaro Mutis, the great gadfly Fernando Vallejo and the witer and sculptor Rodrigo Arenas Betancourt, but those who stayed in Colombia often chose a nearly voluntary marginality: Fernando González, a philosopher who dared to think about the country in terms that ignored the stereotyped guidelines of the West, was a guide for several rebellious generations.

From his unconventional teaching would emerge the defiant writings of Gonzalo Arango, the poet who founded the "Nadaísmo" movement, which was not so much a literary school but, at a time of national discord, a center of great friendships; and the intellectual adventure of Estanislao Zuleta, an impassioned reader, thinker, eloquent and lucid exponent of ideas, teacher of his land and his century.

1958 marked the start of the 16 years of the National Front, an aristocratic conjuration against the degradation of political violence: four presidential terms in which only the candidates of one party stood, in turn, for the presidential elections. This two-party rule coincided with an epoch of relative tranquility, one of the few intervals of decency which Colombia had in the 20th century, and brought the country a minimum stability, but its long-term consequences were ill-fated for Colombian political life and its always fragile democracy.

These governments, which were committed to peaceful coexistence but only among the traditional leaders, did not receive a country where a democratic education had been established, but the heritage of a world made to measure for the party bosses and clergy, and, wary of a democracy that did not seem suitable for the people, maintained their policy of placing severe restrictions on civic rights. Equally wary of free expression and the mobilization of the masses, they made use of a curious mechanism for the periodical suspension of constitutional rights, the so-called "*Estado de sitio*" (literally "State of siege" or martial law).

Omar Rayo, *Shuja II*, 1971, acrylic on canvas, 102 x 102 cm. Banco de la República. Bogotá.

Thus, in a country which needed democracy and pluralism like no other, the official idea that the two traditional parties were the exclusive owners of the State was allowed to prosper and an effective democracy was kept in check. The system wound up forcing many who felt excluded from politics to become indifferent to it and to the tiny social world that upheld that policy, and plunged others into an opposition that, in the absence of rights, turned towards marginality and violence.

These governments should have dealt with the enormous challenge of the disorderly growth of the cities. In fifty years the population of Bogotá rose from 600,000 to nearly eight million inhabitants; that of Medellín from 200,000 to three million; and that of Cali from 150,000 to two million. Poverty began to be apparent in a dramatic way, precisely due to the fact that being poor in the countryside never means being hungry and indigent, while in the cities families may come to lack everything. The contrast between social sectors which had been rooted in urban customs for a long time, in a civic style, and the masses who arrived with their noble peasant traditions, now useless and also despised, sharpened the crisis of exclusion; the ruling class was unable to perceive the enormous sociological change which that violent urbanization brought with it.

Some popular leaders from what was known as the Revolutionary Liberal Movement, like Alfonso Barberena in Cali, warned of the magnitude of the challenges that this accelerated urbanization posed for a country which was unaware of itself, and they bravely fought to establish a place in the urban space and civic conscience for those masses which had lost their niche in history and the support of their myths. The center of interest began to be exclusively the city, but, obsessed with the idea that the city was the future, that modernity was the urban, the country forgot that this rapid urbanization was not the natural result of social evolution but of a dramatic process of expulsion, of a barbaric and primitive blood ritual. It was crime, not progress, which invented those overnight cities.

Beginning with the immense coffee zone, on which the country depended economically and from which a good part of the peasant-farmer population was expelled, the violence had spread to many regions. Later the countryside was gradually abandoned. In the early 60's all you heard about was agrarian reform, but since the 1930's all of the successive bills for agrarian reform had been sunk in a Congress of landowners and they have continued to be sunk up to today. What provoked that discourse was not so much the dramatic situation of the peasant-farmers as the threat posed by the Cuban revolution.

In Colombia room was made for a formal democracy where the important thing was the appearance of legitimacy, not getting those rituals to correspond to profound democratic truths. A corollary to the old juridical style inherited from the colony, which is called "*manzanillismo*" in the country: that is, ensuring a scrupulous respect for the letter of the law but closing your eyes to its social consequences. A rough

Claude Feuillet, *Jungle* (detail), 1979, oil on canvas, 152 x 118.5 cm. Colombian Coffee-Growers Federation. Bogotá.

Pages 282-283: María Cristina Cortés, *Homogeneous landscape* (detail), 1988, oil on canvas. 116 x 163 cm.

Beginning with the immense coffee zone, on which the country depended economically and from which a good part of the peasant-farmer population was expelled, the violence had spread to many regions. Later the countryside was gradually abandoned. In the early 60's all you heard about was agrarian reform, but since the 1930's all of the successive bills for agrarian reform had been sunk in a Congress of landowners and they have continued to be sunk up to today.

Diva Teresa Ramírez, *Ballerinas in space*, 1976, acrylic on paper. 160 x 170 cm. Banco de la República. Bogotá.

dogmatism that made sure that things were legal, whatever the cost, even when their injustice was evident.

A notable example of what that legalistic and manipulative spirit on the part of the usufructuaries of the law consists of was seen in the 1957 plebiscite. The Colombian Constitution had formally been in force since 1886; it was a conservative, centralistic constitution, which ignored the diversity of the country, but its main virtue was that it upheld the principle of a unified country in a territory where there had been so many different indigenous nations before the Conquest, where the idea of a unitary nation had not been strengthened under the Colony and where the Vice-royalty had barely lasted a number of decades. In the second half of the 19th century, federalism tried to interpret the complexity of the country, but in the absence of a prior establishment of a national mentality, it wound up stimulating the secessionist longings of the provincial elites, each desirous of ruling over a small republic adjusted to its interests.

Only the 1886 Constitution came to create and strengthen awareness of a unitary country, even though its unifying element was an aristocratic centralism disdainful of the regions, a patriotic discourse based on a colonial version of history and the fiction of the parties and their powers: the strands of a story that was meant to prove that the old wars and many territorial losses had not been errors but secret victories achieved by the Bogotá aristocracy.

To this was added the superstitious relation to the language, mentioned above, based on the veneration of a pureblooded rigidity, and the mental outlook of feudal landowners allied with a strong and politicized clerical power.

Colombia was and in large measure still is a country where sacred components of our national identity, like the Indians and Blacks, were considered to be degenerate races by official philosophers and excluded from a truly democratic political and educational program. These anti-democratic practices were never questioned by the intellectual elite, nor did they lead to an opportune response from governments which unperturbedly witnessed the dissolution of traditions, even supported violence and exodus at times and in a thousand ways tolerated the demolition of a whole world.

In 1957, to end a military dictatorship that had been imposed by the parties but soon took things into its own hands, the politicians finally resorted to the extreme measure of convoking the citizenry to vote in a plebiscite. Recurring to the illegality of *coup d'état* to smooth over its differences had caused fewer scruples in the Colombian ruling class than having to now recur to the people to legally resolve the problem of the dictatorship and the violence which the same ruling class had unleashed.

This awakened the Colombian ruling class's nearly instinctive fear of anything that reeked of popular power, but they needed to legitimize the aristocratic pact of the National Front in a way that would convince the rest of the world and it was undeniable that in a nominally democratic country such legitimacy would be conferred by the people. Nevertheless, their wariness of the people (or fear of their decision) was

This process of urbanization transformed Colombia. A bucolic country of farmers turned into a licentious country of cities, where all of that enormous diversity, previously dispersed, became clearly evident. The peasant-farmers, who before had lived in lost mountains and valleys, prairies and sierras, deserts of salt and the eternal mists of the Central Massif, were pitched into the unfamiliar life of slums that grew and grew; and in a endless progression that no scholar understood, no politician reformed and no pious soul was able to relieve, the violent Colombianization of the cities of Colombia took place.

so great that the artificers of the plebiscite incorporated a curious clause into it, by which the Colombian people, the same people which now voted, were prohibited from freely expressing themselves through the ballot box again: in other words, they were perpetually banned from then on from making use of the very plebiscite mechanism they now consecrated. *Manzanillismo* thus added new pen strokes to its own caricature. The National Front arose, at one and the same time, as an aristocratic pact and a gag which the populace, manipulated by the politicians, imposed on itself. Many years later, the purity of the norm would have to be violated to be able to hold the plebiscite that opened the way for the 1991 Constituent Assembly, which drafted the Constitution that has governed the country since then.

It is worth pointing out that each presidential period of the National Front left the country with a new social conflict. The government of Alberto Lleras Camargo witnessed the formal emergence of the FARC guerrilla army. The government of Guillermo León Valencia, an affable politician from Cauca and son of the modernist poet Guillermo Valencia, fond of epigrams and hunting, witnessed the appearance of the EPL guerrilla army. And as a result of the election of Misael Pastrana Borrero, a radical sector of the youth movements of the Alianza Nacional Popular (National Popular Alliance) founded, in the cities, the M-19 guerrilla force.

Later, during that astonishing prolongation of the National Front that was the government of Alfonso López Michelsen, there began the boom in narcotics-trafficking and government corruption, and from there on Colombia witnessed the growth of new illegal armies, dissident guerrilla groups, peasant-farmer self-defense movements and the "popular militias" of the cities. The guerrilla armies in question had grown out of small and localized groups, remnants of the political violence of the 1950's whose origins were in the traditional centers of conflict, or they were the offspring of Communist dissidences or the Cuban Revolution: in all cases they were the product of the exclusion that ruled over our society. To begin with, they were vehemently branded as criminal gangs by the government and the communications media, but now, decades later, those same powers reproach them for no longer being romantic fighters for justice, for having abandoned their ideals.

The social background against which such developments stood out was the dramatic transformation of Colombia into an urban reality without a clear industrial vocation but with the countryside in ruins. Ever since the mid-19th century and in a continual way, the peasant-farmer economy had been based on the growing of coffee, which wound up being the only form of small-scale agriculture that withstood, a little, the implacable annihilation of the smallholder in the name of a supposed profitability that nevertheless impoverished the poor. Colombia lived off coffee and managed to produce one whose quality was unique in the world, thanks in part to its special varieties. But above all, it was due to the system of cultivation and processing taught to the producers by the National Federation of Coffee-Growers. Perhaps there is no

Elsa Zambrano, picture from *"The schools"* series, 1979, acrylic on canvas, 120 x 110 cm. Suramericana de Seguros Collection.

1958 marked the start of the 16 years of the National Front, an aristocratic conjuration against the degradation of political violence: four presidential terms in which only the candidates of one party stood, in turn, for the presidential elections. This two-party rule coincided with an epoch of relative tranquility, one of the few intervals of decency which Colombia had in the 20th century, and brought the country a minimum stability, but its long-term consequences were ill-fated for Colombian political life and its always fragile democracy.

other product that has to go through so many stages from the moment it is sown to the moment when it is consumed.

Processes of planting, picking, washing, depulping, drying, threshing, selection, toasting and grinding – all of which are needed to arrive at the final beverage – make coffee one of the most culturally-elaborated natural products in the world and it is a pity that Colombia, which learned to grow it with a special care and talent, has not been able to perfect the final processes, which are those which give the highest value to the final product, nor learned to become a country of discriminating consumers either. You could say that coffee provides the clearest example of the irrationality of a world that produces refinement for others but is incapable of enjoying that refinement itself.

In the rest of the countryside there was a growing effort to strengthen agro-industry alone: the great plantations of sugar cane that fed the sugar mills in the Valle del Cauca; the fields of cotton and fruit in the central valleys; the northern regions devoted to the growing of bananas. The natural vocation of half of Colombian territory is the tropical forest, which supplies water and oxygen to a planet that desperately needs them. Of the rest of our territory, 17 million hectares are known to be apt for agriculture and 9 million for cattle-rearing.

Nevertheless, the amount of land given over to agricultural production has dramatically shrunk, while that devoted to intensive cattle-farming has irrationally increased. Even graver, many absentee-owned properties are not productive nor subject to any system of taxation.

The guerrilla armies were an expression, above all, of the marginal sectors of the peasant-farmer population, although the ELN, which arose under the influence of the Cuban revolution, had been strengthened by the adherence of young university students and intellectuals. The most prominent of all was the priest Camilo Torres Restrepo, an idealistic sociologist who attempted to lead a movement of opposition to the National Front, but was so antagonized by the intolerance of the powers that be that he wound up becoming a symbol of the revolutionary struggle in Latin America, only surpassed later on by Che Guevara.

Camilo Torres Restrepo had participated in the writing of the book *La violencia en Colombia*, which was a heart-rending summary, from an academic outlook, of the violence which the Liberal and Conservative parties had patronized between 1944 and 1964. Convinced, like Gaitán, that the two parties were the ruin of the country, he founded the *Frente Unido* (United Front) but desperation and the persecution of his movement threw him into the arms of the guerrilla and even led him to believe, like others, that the insurrection of the Colombian people was imminent.

But the violence of the 1950's had been a real civil war, in the sense that Colombians, manipulated from speaker's platforms and pulpits and the victim of their own ancestral memory, considered the triumph of their respective party to be their own salvation.

Opposite:
Noé León, *The tigress* (detail), 1967, oil on cardboard. 39 x 72 cm. Banco de la República. Bogotá.

Pages 290-291:
Delcy Morelos, *Paradigms of the burned being* (detail), 1994, acrylic on paper, 161 x 164 cm. Banco de la República. Bogotá.

In Colombia room was made for a formal democracy where the important thing was the appearance of legitimacy, not getting those rituals to correspond to profound democratic truths. A corollary to the old juridical style inherited from the colony, which is called "manzanillismo" in the country: that is, ensuring a scrupulous respect for the letter of the law but closing your eyes to its social consequences.

Guillermo Wiedemann, *Assemblage*, 1963, collage. 72 x 72 cm.

This spirit of worshipping the letter of the law but being indifferent to justice is typical of societies in which the cult of appearances and respect for authority are important, not the triumph of intelligence or truth, where it is always safer to repeat than to innovate, to follow orders than to assume responsibilities.

Once the violence had been overcome, even if it was only for a brief time, the community accepted the reconciliation of the National Front as an accomplished fact and believed that Colombia was at peace. We Colombians were tired of violence and it was the moment to create new parties to modernize and pacify the country. But Camilo Torres was able to prove how difficult such an attempt was, because the powers that be in Colombia, alarmed by the Cuban Revolution, saw communism in all expressions of the opposition and decided to deny any possibility of legal political expression to those who showed their opposition to the model they had established. Camilo Torres Restrepo's adherence to the guerrilla movement helped to give it a fleeting intellectual prestige and his destiny was the same as that of the poet José Martí in Cuba during the struggle for independence: both died on their first day of combat.

This took place in the 1960's and Colombian youth, suddenly plunged into the turbulent urban peace, was divided between those who felt a growing anguish about a dark future and those who welcomed the arrival of the modernity that began to let the fresh air of the world into the country. The military regime of Gustavo Rojas Pinilla was partly responsible for those winds of change: he mounted social campaigns to help the poor and built a number of roads in a country whose network of highways was incredibly precarious. New wave and rock music took advantage of the television which had been recently inaugurated by Rojas Pinilla and the younger generation gave it an enthusiastic welcome. A new generation of Colombian novelists flourished at that time, like Héctor Rojas Herazo, Álvaro Cepeda Samudio, Manuel Zapata Olivella and Gabriel García Márquez. In poetry there was the always youthful León de Greiff, Aurelio Arturo, Meira del Mar, Álvaro Mutis, and Jorge Gaitán Durán, as well as "nadaístas" like Jaime Jaramillo Escobar and Jotamario Arbeláez.

Then there was the explosion of young artists, represented by figures like Édgar Negret, Eduardo Ramírez Villamizar, Fernando Botero, Alejandro Obregón, Luis Caballero, Margarita Lozano, Enrique Grau, Lucy and Hernando Tejada and Feliza Bursztyn, and the even younger Carlos Granada and Ana Mercedes Hoyos. All this took place in the midst of the debates provoked by the well-informed and polemical Argentinean art critic Marta Traba, whose impassioned and sometimes unjust rankings shook the provincial ambient of Colombian art out of its traditional lethargy. Traba founded the Bogotá Museum of Modern Art, while there flourished at the same time the renovating theatrical enterprises of great maestros like Enrique Buenaventura and Santiago García, as well as the memorable literary reviews *Mito* and *Eco*.

Towards the end of the National Front, the ex–dictator Gustavo Rojas Pinilla tried to gather the votes of those who were opposed to the two parties and become a third force in the political debate, but, even though everyone believes today that he won the 1970 elections, there was a sudden final upsurge in the votes for the Conservative candidate Misael Pastrana. Rojas Pinilla, who had chosen, in 1957, to withdraw his candidacy instead of appealing to the people and precipitating a civil war, renounced

his ambitions for the second time, sacrificing, in this case, the hopes of more than a million voters.

This frustration led to the emergence of the M-19 guerrilla movement, mostly made up of young intellectuals from the cities, which grew throughout the following twenty years, thanks to the audacity of its military actions and flair for publicity, and came to have a certain romantic appeal for the middle classes of the country. It reached an ideological plenitude with the emergence into public life of Jaime Bateman, who seemed to have overcome the doctrinaire fanaticism of the Colombian *guerrilleros* and aimed at the inclusion of broader sectors of the population. This discourse was joined to an intensification of the group's military actions, but Bateman died in a mysterious air crash on his way to Panama and his movement never got over his loss.

The irruption into national life of narcotics-trafficking added a new and dramatic element to politics and seemed to exclude the possibility that a political movement which recurred to arms would be able to change society.

In 1974, when the 16 year period agreed on by the National Front came to an end, Alfonso López Michelsen came to power, a politician who had originally been one of the strongest critics of that anti-democratic pincer movement. Paradoxically, his government, which should have led the country's transition to constitutional liberties and an active democracy, persisted in the habits of the regime of restricted rights. It allowed the destruction of natural resources to continue; witnessed, with impotence or indifference, the growing power of the narcotics-traffickers; opened the doors to widespread corruption in the administration, and, as with previous governments, continued to be hostile to all democratic opposition.

The scenario of democracy remained the same as in the three previous lustrums: peasant-farmer, student and workers movements were energetically rebuffed; the right to strike was practically banned, while the media depicted it as a sign of the malignity of labor; the struggles by students for a more democratic and modern educational system ran up against an authoritarianism that was unable to enter into any kind of dialogue and this strengthened the conviction of the armed movements that the only alternative was war. Alfonso López Michelsen, the former critic of the system, wound up becoming the canonical voice of the old country, which rewarded with a limitless respect and the legend of a prodigious intellect his final adherence to the order against which he had fought.

Another consequence of the National Front was the complete closure of opportunities for middle class entrepreneurs. The emergence of the M-19 was a good example of the way in which some sectors of the middle class felt choked by the existing legal framework and failed to find opportunities for political expression in the field of that restricted democracy. At the beginning of the 1970's, stimulated by a growing international market, a number of Colombian smugglers began to turn to drugs trafficking. The youth movement of the sixties had paved the way in different parts of

Lorenzo Jaramillo, *Faces* (detail), 1981, pastel on paper, 100 x 70 cm.

The youth movement of the sixties had paved the way in different parts of the world for the widespread consumption of natural stimulants like marijuana, as well as manufactured substances like LSD and other psychoactives, and the United States reacted to it by reviving one of its most pathetic campaigns: prohibition.

Opposite:
Juan Antonio Roda,
The color of light
(detail), 2000, oil on
canvas. 125 x 150 cm.

Pages 298-299:
Édgar Negret,
Calendar (detail),
1995, painted
aluminum.
161 x 161 x 40 cm.

*This took place in the
1960's and Colombian
youth, suddenly plunged
into the turbulent urban
peace, was divided
between those who felt a
growing anguish about
a dark future and those
who welcomed the arrival
of the modernity that
began to let the fresh air
of the world into the
country.*

the world for the widespread consumption of natural stimulants like marijuana, as well as manufactured substances like LSD and other psychoactives, and the United States reacted to it by reviving one of its most pathetic campaigns: prohibition.

It should have foreseen that, as always occurs, such a strategy would stimulate the development of a lucrative market, but it seems that at the beginning of that decade no one seriously thought that that business would turn into an industry of gigantic proportions. In Colombia the traffickers were seen as a variety of contrabandist, lucky ones, and for many people they were a caricature nouveau riche because of their ostentation, doubtful architectural and decorative taste and their tendency to imitate the style of Americans. Neither the government nor ordinary people understood that they were witnessing the emergence of the first great multinational partly controlled by Latin Americans.

Most of all, no one imagined that the public which consumed psychoactive substances in the industrialized countries would be so large nor that it would be willing to invest so much money to satisfy its addiction to drugs. The situation of Colombia was especially favorable to the appearance of traffickers. Colombian history was a long chronicle of productive efforts which had only been successful in the case of products acceptable to the mother countries. It was for that reason that our continent witnessed the establishment of sugar republics, banana republics, cattle republics and coffee republics: it was the metropolis which imposed the logic of production and our peasant-farmers were always dependant on its market power. Beyond this, the Colombian economy was always structured round the production of luxury goods or those which came to have the characteristics of luxuries and nearly vices. Gold, pearls, emeralds, tobacco and coffee, successively, were some of the major export goods of the Colombian market and many of these bonanzas provoked a peculiar violence.

If the governments of the metropolises and our countries had been aware, before it became too late, of the potential violence associated with those immensely lucrative clandestine enterprises, they might have taken measures to prevent this danger by stimulating not only the production but also the consumption of other agricultural products which would have stopped the narcotics boom.

There were times in the past when coffee and chocolate came to be regarded as addictive drugs so dangerous that they were prohibited in many societies. Alcohol, which is legally consumed today even though it is an undeniable cause of accidents and fatal diseases, was fiercely prohibited in certain epochs and the main effect of that prohibition was the formation of extraordinarily violent criminal groups. The coca leaf is a natural product that has been consumed by the indigenous peoples of America for millennia: it has formed part of their religious rites and been a tool for their knowledge. Cocaine, for its part, that is, the industrial powder derived from the coca leaf, was a product which European society tolerated and consumed in the second half of the 19th century: it achieved the status of a refined luxury, like snuff,

Colombia was and in large measure still is a country where sacred components of our national identity, like the Indians and Blacks, were considered to be degenerate races by official philosophers and excluded from a truly democratic political and educational program. "Indio" and "negro" became insults, just as the venerable word "montañero" (highlander) did in the 1950´s, coming to mean, in a country of mountains, all that was rude, primitive and naïve. These anti-democratic practices were never questioned or criticized by the intellectual elite, nor did they lead to an opportune response from governments…

and intellectuals like Sigmund Freud consumed it on a fairly regular basis and their interest in it led to important scientific discoveries. In the late 19th and early 20th centuries, French cafés were full of posters advertising liqueurs derived from coca, which became very popular. Many affirm that what really stimulated the current cocaine bonanza was prohibition, and this was pointed out as far back as 1979, when the problem was barely beginning to be apparent, by the most important intellectual in the Colombian establishment, Alberto Lleras Camargo, the first president under the National Front.

What we do know is that, well before governments became aware of it, the trafficking of marijuana and cocaine had turned into a gigantic business, and the apparently inoffensive dealers had become enormously rich and powerful men. Since it could not be regulated by law and the courts, the clandestine economy which had brought them great fortunes was necessarily based on the bloody resort to private justice, vendettas, the accumulation of military power and terrorism. From the beginning of this process the authorities indiscriminately blamed the three distinct sectors which participate in the drugs business: the poor peasant-farmers who grow the leaf, for whom sowing and harvesting coca, as their ancestors did, is a normal activity of agricultural subsistence; sectors of the middle class who, at a time of economic crisis, seek to benefit from the circulation of drugs money in a thousand different ways; and the great mafias of traffickers, which are only partly made up of Latin American adventurers, since there is no doubt that the big distributors, who manage most of the business at a stage when the merchandise has its highest value, operate in the nations where the drug is consumed.

The peasant-farmers with a threatened subsistence economy do not understand why a plant that was always sacred for the indigenous people should be categorized as the embodiment of evil by a foolish civilization and its cultivation condemned as a criminal activity, and even more so when you consider that the main Coca-Cola plant, in Atlanta, was always a major legal buyer of coca leaves. It might be better to ask ourselves why the most widespread legal product of the consumer society in the industrial age and its most persecuted illegal product both mysteriously come from the same plant.

At the beginning of the 1980's, the drugs traffickers began to turn to politics. Carlos Lehder had founded a nationalistic party with a strange ideology, the National Latin Movement, and the then nearly unknown trafficker Pablo Escobar Gaviria had got himself elected to the House of Representatives. They soon wanted to have candidates for the presidency of the republic. It was then that their relationship with the government got tense. The United States suddenly seemed to become aware that the drugs fortunes were gigantic, consumption had shot up and the subterranean power of the drugs lords was something to be reckoned with. It didn't take long for the war against narcotics-trafficking to be declared. The response of the traffickers to this

Ana Mercedes Hoyos, *Bazurto I* series (detail), 1992, oil on canvas, 150 x 150 cm.

war and to the threat of extradition to the United States was terrorism and there thus began the next episode in the interminable violence of Colombia.

The cartel of Gonzalo Rodríguez Gacha and Pablo Escobar began to wage a ruthless war against society and the government which left thousands of victims in a matter of a few years. The poverty-stricken slums, which had received no benefits from the State and were the home of the offspring of those who had gone through the violence of the 1950's – youngsters without education or horizons to whom no one gave a helping hand – became the breeding ground of hired killers paid for by the narcotics fortunes. Hundreds of poor, aimless youngsters turned into implacable executioners at the service of those criminal bands and a new ideology, based on the idea that easy money and violence were the only ways to win respect, took hold of the cities of Colombia.

By the beginning of the 1980's it was already clear that something grave was happening to the institutional order of Colombia. The political parties had lost their former influence and their ability to mount opposition, but some old-style leaders still acted as a check on their moral decomposition. Nevertheless, the National Front had already carried out its mission of taking the country apart. The masses were overwhelmed by resentment, education had never been a government priority, poverty necessarily turned into a factory for the production of delinquents and narcotics-trafficking took shape as an enormous power that wanted political recognition, above all.

Representatives of the drugs lords met with some public figures in Panama and made an astonishing proposal: they were willing to pay the country's national debt and give up the business in exchange for the right be judged for their crimes in Colombia and doubtless obtain a legal amnesty for a part of their fortunes. The offer implied either winning the agreement of the international community – a difficult matter – or defying it, and president Belisario Betancur flatly refused to enter into that negotiation, which even politicians like López Michelsen and intellectuals like Gabriel García Márquez thought feasible. That was the moment when it might have been possible, perhaps, to dismember the nascent mafias, for they had yet to embrace terrorism and the persistence of the Cold War had not yet turned the war against drugs into the main priority of the world's strongest empire.

But the drugs lords had already created a kind of turbid mythology. Their immense properties, which gave a single family ownership of a nearly a million hectares; their stables of Colombian *paso fino* horses; their inaccessible strongholds; their plane routes to the coasts of the United States; their private islands in the Caribbean; their love stories; their brutal crimes; their populist gestures, like the construction of well-equipped sports centers and street lights in districts that had suffered from government negligence for decades; their barrels stuffed full of dollars that seemed to revive the legendary buried treasures of the pre-Colombian cultures in a post-modernist context; their Ferraris and Alfa Romeos – all of it engendered a chorus of rumors that entranced the youngsters of the slums.

José Freddy Serna, *Evening north*, 1997, 160 x 150 cm, oil on canvas. Suramericana de Seguros Collection.

The contrast between social sectors which had been rooted in urban customs for a long time, in a civic style, and the masses who arrived with their noble peasant traditions, now useless and also despised, sharpened the crisis of exclusion; the ruling class was unable to perceive the enormous sociological change which that violent urbanization brought with it.

Typical of it all was the hacienda Nápoles in Doradal in the Magdalena valley, owned by Pablo Escobar, on the gateway of which was mounted the light plane which, rumor had it, had carried his first shipment of drugs to the United States. Once inside, the visitor would see the bullet-riddled Bentley that had supposedly belonged to a U.S. gangster and an extensive garden with exotic animals freely-ranging over the pastureland. Whole villages suddenly sprang up alongside the highways near those great estates and forests of buildings rose in the main cities of Colombia. New cities grew up in the old ones during those fifteen years: the construction industry had a surprising boom and Colombia enjoyed an inexplicable economic stability at the very time that the rest of the continent seemed to be plunged into recession.

Colombia, a country which had never lived through the splendor of Mexico in colonial times or Havana at the end of the eighteenth century or Argentina at the beginning of the twentieth century, enjoyed for few years a vague imitation of such prosperity, which even extended to certain sectors of the poor classes. It was only that its cause, which Colombian governments more than once attributed to their sound economic policy, was no more than a reflection of a violent clandestine business to which the empire paid enormous amounts of money. Some Colombian traffickers even appeared on the annual list of the world's richest men published by *Forbes* magazine.

But the assassination of the Minister of Justice, Rodrigo Lara, in 1984 and the government's application of the extradition treaty that was in force with the United States gave rise to a terrorist war that kept Colombia in a state of turmoil for the next ten years and the war with the *extraditables* (those liable to be extradited) brought the country a succession bombings, bomb threats, political kidnappings and murders of political leaders.

In 1985 a commando force of the M-19 guerrilla assaulted the Supreme Court building and took judges, workers and members of the public as hostages. An autonomous decision by the generals, which was later authorized by the president, led the army to retake the building by fire and sword but the operation only wound up immolating many of the hostages. It began with a symbolic image, the spectacle of the weapons of the republic being turned against the doors of justice, a gesture which seemed to presage the collapse of the legal order before the advance of armed force.

It was also at that time, in response to a proposal for political negotiations with the guerrilla groups, led by the Betancur administration and aimed at the re-incorporation of the rebels into civilian life as members of a democratic opposition, that an attempt was made to found a left-wing political movement, the Unión Patriótica. Incredibly, more than three thousand unarmed members of that party were assassinated in an implacable process that seemed to exhaust the Colombian guerrilla groups' willingness to enter into political negotiations that might lead to peace. In successive waves of terrorism, four presidential candidates, several ministers and high government officials, numerous judges and members of the armed forces were assassinated dur-

Opposite:
David Manzur,
St. George defeated (detail), 1993,
pastel on paper.
50 x 65 cm.

Pages 306-307:
Eduardo Ramírez Villamizar, *Sculpture*.

Some popular leaders from what was known as the Revolutionary Liberal Movement, like Alfonso Barberena in Cali, warned of the magnitude of the challenges that this accelerated urbanization posed for a country which was unaware of itself, and they bravely fought to establish a place in the urban space and civic conscience for those masses which had lost their niche in history and the support of their myths.

Miguel Ángel Rojas, *Jaguar* (detail), 1999, oil and gold leaf on canvas. 140 x 175 cm.

In the face of a weak State, riddled with corruption, the private armies grew stronger and in many regions the irregular nature of the war led the arms of the republic to be turned against its laws.

ing the administration of Virgilio Barco and the explosion of bombs in public places turned some Colombian cities into a nightmare.

We might say that wars in Colombia neither begin nor end: they simply go through a transformation. The war between Liberals and Conservatives in the 1950's turned into the silent war against any opposition in the following years and later into the war provoked by the early guerrilla armies. Then came the war of the M-19 and while it was still going on, the terrorist war of the narcotics-traffickers broke out. In the 1980's, it was thought that life would turn into a bed of roses if the country were to rid itself of Gonzalo Rodríguez Gacha and Pablo Escobar, but after the first had been killed in a plantain grove in the Caribbean and the other shot to death on a rooftop in Medellín, the next war, more violent and generalized, took its place. In the face of a weak State, riddled with corruption, the private armies grew stronger.

Strengthened by the debilitation of the State and feeding off kidnapping, extortion, what were known as *vacunas* (literally vaccines, meaning protection money), and "taxes" paid by the narcotics-traffickers, the FARC guerrilla army grew and spread through the whole country. Also devoted to kidnapping, as well as attacks on the electricity infrastructure, the ELN guerrilla likewise extended its control over certain parts of the country, while the EPL, in turn, kept up the war in some regions. As a response to this upsurge of the guerrilla, there was a corresponding growth in rural self-defense groups, determined to protect regions with medium-sized family farms and agro-businesses which the government had left unprotected. There were also paramilitary groups which went on the offensive: they set out to wage an irregular war against the guerrillas and did not hesitate to sow terror in the countryside and rural towns. Meanwhile, the so-called "popular militias" came to dominate many districts in the cities.

The Colombian Army, which often saw itself accused of tolerating violations of human rights by those in its ranks, found it difficult to respond on so many different fronts. Sectors of the threatened society demanded that the Army protect them and even pressured the Army to employ illegal practices to defend their interests. There thus became generalized attacks on towns, the taking of prisoners in order to exchange them for those held by the other side, kidnappings for the purpose of ransom, including the random ones at road-blocks of the kind the guerrillas called *pescas milagrosas* (fishing for miracles), selective massacres and the assassination of leaders of democratic organizations, under the pretext that they belonged to one of the opposing bands. He who refused to participate in the war might be accused of belonging to the opposite side by any of the bands, even though none of these factions awakened the enthusiasm of the population nor formulated a civilized and coherent proposal for a better future.

The traditional system of privilege had strengthened a kind of economic protectionism that tolerated negligence and the production of shoddy goods by those who benefited from government favor. Under the pretext of correcting this mistake, the

Colombia will not be able to attain the benefits of modernity if it does not dare to look at itself in the mirror of its own complexity and if it not does allow each citizen the right to exercise his freedom and receive his measure of responsibility. This depends only in part on the existing State. It depends, above all, on a new citizenry that is capable of great decisions, original economic and social initiatives, and cultural and educational programs that would turn us into a nation which is reconciled with its memory, territory and originality.

government of César Gaviria decreed an indiscriminate opening-up of the economy at the beginning of the 1990's, which, instead of strengthening the economy by improving the quality of goods and competitive capacity and supporting Colombian producers, handed the market over to an invasion of goods from economies that were better organized and precipitated the ruin of immense sectors of industry and agriculture. The same government brought the political negotiations with the M-19 guerrilla to a happy end, which paved the way for the convocation of a National Constituent Assembly in 1991 that put an end to the rule of the centenary Constitution of Miguel Antonio Caro and Rafael Núñez and seemed to breathe new life into the strangled Colombian democracy.

The following government set out to moderate the disastrous effects of the *apertura* (the "opening" or liberalization of the economy), but the scandal provoked by the financing of president Ernesto Samper's campaign with drugs money subjected his government to so much political pressure that, to avoid resigning from office, he invested a good part of the budget in buying off the electorate through publicity campaigns and populist gestures, and, at the behest of the United States, declared a war without mercy against drugs money. As the economy deteriorated and the State, a victim of its own corruption, grew weaker under these governments, the private armies of the left and right became stronger, to the point where the regular army was unable to control them at times.

It is an inexorable vicious circle: since the State, subject to private interests and privileged circles, cannot provide solutions to the problems of the countryside, the guerrilla armies arise. Since it cannot find economic solutions for the poor in the cities either, crime is strengthened. As a result of this and since the State is not in a condition to protect the urban and rural middle classes from the guerrilla and crime, the paramilitaries and private vigilante armies come into being.

But since the State's defense budget has to be invested in the war against the rebels and the mafias, investment in social welfare declines: citizens increasingly become victims of poverty, unemployment, ignorance and criminal gangs, and the cities turn into a no man's land. Thus, a single cause, the loss of State legitimacy, has endless consequences that are chaotic for the whole community, and Colombia continues to be torn apart by a crisis that has more heads than the mythical Hydra, without knowing how to even begin to deal with it.

In 1998, president Andrés Pastrana met with the guerrilla leader Manuel Marulanda in the mountains of Colombia and started a peace process which initially reawakened the hopes of a community that was fed up with violence, full of mistrust and had nearly completely lost the free use of its territory. The government based its program on a political negotiation that would lead to an armistice with the insurgent armies. With this aim in mind, it undertook serious political risks, like turning the area of five large municipalities into a "no-go" zone for the armed forces in order to advance the

Fabián Rendón, *Winds* (detail), undated, linoleum engraving on paper. 70.2 x 100 cm. Banco de la República. Bogotá.

Luis Luna, *picture from the "Desastres de Goya" series*, 1999, oil on canvas. 140 x 150 cm.

What we do know is that, well before governments became aware of it, the trafficking of marijuana and cocaine had turned into a gigantic business, and the apparently inoffensive dealers had become enormously rich and powerful men. Since it could not be regulated by law and the courts, the clandestine economy which had brought them great fortunes was necessarily based on the bloody resort to private justice, vendettas, the accumulation of military power and terrorism.

negotiations that went on there, at a time when the rest of the country remained at war. The government also expressly accepted that the guerrilla was a political organization, had a program and was a valid interlocutor of the government; and gradually agreed to a series of procedural conditions as well as a common agenda shared by the insurgents. At the beginning of 2001 a similar process began to be sketched out with the ELN guerrilla force.

Nevertheless, by the following year everything had changed: the negotiations with the guerrilla were broken off and the same electorate which had voted for Andrés Pastrana in the hope that he would negotiate a peace now voted for Álvaro Uribe Vélez so that he would wage an unlimited war against the insurgents. Despite the apparent concessions which the two sides had made, what most persisted, in one camp and the other, was a distrust that had become chronic after decades of unyielding war. For Uribe's government the guerrillas were terrorist organization that had to be forced to negotiate by means of a military harassment that would require a large investment of money.

One of the main demands made by the guerrilla armies during the negotiations was the extinction of the paramilitary groups which had become their main enemy in recent years, although they were also an enemy of the law and the legitimacy of the State. Uribe initiated negotiations with the paramilitaries, which suggests that he is willing to negotiate with all the subversive groups, but only on the basic condition of a verifiable ceasefire.

Uribe's security strategy made people feel that it was safe to travel on the highways again, stimulated investment and gave his government an unprecedented level of popularity in opinion polls. This encouraged his followers and the government itself to call for his reelection. However, the permanence of these achievements depends on a continued investment in security which would only enable the government to keep the insurgents at bay at the cost of postponing urgent social investments and considerably increasing the country's debt, or a political negotiation that would restore the State's capacity to act in the social and economic fields.

It is not that the Colombian state is particularly inept. The Spanish army has been fighting the ETA for decades and the powerful British army has not been able to destroy the IRA. In the case of Colombia, however, it is a matter of veritable armies scattered throughout a country whose topography makes the strongholds in which they fight nearly impregnable.

But the citizenry should not have too many illusions that a dialogue between the warring bands would give it the gift of a more civilized country. The only thing that the armistice might achieve is to create a climate of peace favorable to great transformations. Thus, the real solution lies in the formation of a national democratic movement committed to the country and its future, which emphatically refuses to perpetuate the political style of the traditional parties or use violence as a solution for our problems.

The first task is to recognize the now evident complexity of the country and renew its institutions accordingly. We must modify its political habits, make all citizens equal before the law, seek a true national solidarity and give dignity to the community. There can be no democracy without democrats, without a community that has sufficient maturity to oversee the governments it elects. Transformations cannot take place when governments do not represent an ethical program, a clear majority will, and thus lack the power to comply with accords in a country which has a long experience of peace agreements breaking down as soon as they were signed.

There can be no educational revolution without a redefinition of national ideals, without overcoming the prejudice and narrow-mindedness which ruled politics for decades. Colombia will not be able to attain the benefits of modernity if it does not dare to look at itself in the mirror of its own complexity and if it not does allow each citizen the right to exercise his freedom and receive his measure of responsibility. This depends only in part on the existing State. It depends, above all, on a new citizenry that is capable of great decisions, original economic and social initiatives, and cultural and educational programs that would turn us into a nation which is reconciled with its memory, territory and originality. Only when every citizen understands that his own role is fundamental will Colombia come out on top.

Opposite:
Carlos Jacanamijoy,
Sunday 4.30 pm
(detail), 2003,
150 x 170 cm.

Below: Fernando Botero, *July 20* (detail), 1984, oil on canvas. 191 x 144 cm. National Museum of Colombia.

Pages 316-317:
Taganga, Magdalena.

Pages 318-319:
San Felipe Castle.
Cartagena, Bolívar.

Pages 320-321:
International Theater Festival. Bogotá.

Transformations cannot take place when governments do not represent an ethical program, a clear majority will...

INDEX OF PHOTOGRAPHERS

Luis Ángel Arango Library Archive: 134-135, 144, 278, 282-283, 284, 289, 290-291, 310.
Carlos Humberto Arango: 138-139, 316-317, back cover.
Jorge Eduardo Arango: 36-37, 56, 68abcd, 204-205, 250.
Juan Fernando Barreto: 270-271.
Eduardo Bonelo: 12-13, 69.
Aldo Brando: 2, 3, 18, 22, 28, 32, 33, 45, 46, 58, 59, 60b, 61, 96, 141, 150, 152, 180, 187, 198-199, 228-229, 249, 258-259, 269, 212-213.
Felipe Caicedo: 85d, 112-113, 124d, 120b.
Antonio Castañeda: 89, 98, 166-167.
Ian Flórez: 48.
Diego Miguel Garcés: 49ac, 52, 53abcd, 54bcd, 55, 62, 66d, 151, 194b, 197, 201a, 202, 261, 262-263.
Camilo Gómez: 282-283.
Pilar Gómez: 50c, 74, 91, 92-93, 292.

Eduardo González: 238.
Enrique Grau Archive: 76-77.
Santiago Harker: 10, 20-21, 40-41, 67, 110, 215, 241, 286.
Jeremy Horner: 24, 25, 39abc, 60ad, 71, 72-73, 84, 85abc, 86, 88, 89, 111, 135, 124abc, 154, 155, 170-171, 189, 190-191, 201b, 206, 219, 237, 254-255, 121b, 257, 264, 266, 267.
Carlos Hoyos: 226ab.
Andrés Hurtado: 26, 45ab, 195b, 220-221.
Benjamín Jacanamijoy Archive: 314.
Luis Luna Archive: 313.
José Fernando Machado: 36-37, 50abd, 66ab, 51, 56, 94, 117, 1181a, 121a, 149, 158-159, 119.
Marko Modic: 44a, 118b, 146, 186, 200a, 318-319.
Óscar Monsalve: 132abc, 177, 178, 230, 297, 274-175, 272, 294, 298-299, 303, 309.

Museo Nacional Archive: 162-163, 315.
Olga Lucía Novoa: 97.
Sylvia Patiño: 79.
Sandra Peña: 118.
Gerardo Reichel-Dolmatoff: 70, 82.
Mario Rivera: 278.
Cristóbal von Rothkirch: 15, 29, 31, 39d, 42, 44b, 45a, 54a, 64, 65, 80-81, 107, 108-109, 116, 120a, 129, 131, 132d, 136, 142-143, 169, 174-175, 182-183, 184, 195a, 200b, 208-209, 210, 222, 225, 232, 233, 234, 240, 242-243, 246, 247, 277, 320-321, front cover.
Miguel Salazar: 66c, 156, 253.
Juan Camilo Segura: 103.
Rudolf Schrimpff: 114.
Cristina Uribe: 194a.
Jesus Vélez: 49d.
Villegas Editores Archive: 60c, 100-101, 104, 105, 133, 147, 160, 164, 172, 216, 244, 281, 306-307.